King Arthur's Children

A Study in Fiction and Tradition

Tyler R. Tichelaar, Ph.D.

The Reflections of Camelot Series

Modern History Press

Modern History Press, an imprint of Loving Healing Press
5145 Pontiac Trail
Ann Arbor, MI 48105

www.ModernHistoryPress.com
info@ModernHistoryPress.com
Tollfree (USA/CAN): 888-761-6268
London, England: 44-20-331-81304

Library of Congress Cataloging-in-Publication Data

Tichelaar, Tyler, 1971-
    King Arthur's children : a study in fiction and tradition / Tyler R. Tichelaar.
        p. cm. -- (The reflections of Camelot series)
    Includes bibliographical references and index.
    ISBN-13: 978-1-61599-066-5 (trade paper : alk. paper)
    ISBN-10: 1-61599-066-6 (trade paper : alk. paper)
    ISBN-13: 978-1-61599-067-2 (hardcover : alk. paper)
    ISBN-10: 1-61599-067-4 (hardcover : alk. paper)
    1. Arthurian romances--History and criticism. 2. Arthur, King--In literature. 3. Children in literature. I. Title.
    PN686.A7T53 2011
    809'.93551--dc22
                                                            2010038116

Distributed by Ingram Book Group, Bertram's Books (UK), Hachette Livre (FR), Agapea (SP), Angus & Robertson (AU).

Contents

Figures

Introduction

The subject of King Arthur's children is not widely known even to the legend's most avid readers. Mention of these children may make readers pause for a moment, say to themselves, "What children?" and then add, "Well, of course there's Mordred, but sometimes he is King Arthur's nephew rather than his son."

My reaction was similar when I first found mention of King Arthur having any children other than Mordred. The fact is, however, that King Arthur has traditionally had children almost since the legends were first told. Over the centuries, these children were lost amid the continually increasing number of new stories, many springing up without any source in the tradition, only to be added to the legend, while the original Celtic stories were largely forgotten. Occasionally, when scholars came across obscure references to one of Arthur's children in the earlier sources, they were unsure what to make of this curiosity. As Arthurian studies have progressed, particularly over the last century, however, efforts have been made to understand the historical time period in which King Arthur lived, around the fifth to early sixth centuries; this research has resulted in many discoveries and even more theories, some of which will now allow us to make more accurate statements about King Arthur's forgotten children.

With the continual increase of interest in the Arthurian legends, it is time that a study finally be made of King Arthur's children. If we wish to discover who the historical King Arthur was, perhaps we might find out something about him by studying his children. The need to study King Arthur's children is almost as important as the study of King Arthur himself because King Arthur's children, as we will see, are what help connect us to King Arthur's time period. The concept of King Arthur and the golden age he established fulfills a psychological yearning for many people. Comfort and satisfaction can be derived from believing in King Arthur's ethical code. People have a need to believe in a golden age as we saw during John F. Kennedy's presidency when attempts were made to compare Kennedy and the United States to King Arthur and Camelot. By discovering Arthur's children and descendants, we find a link between the age of Arthur and our own time.

At the end of *The Discovery of King Arthur*, Geoffrey Ashe asks why the spell of King Arthur continues to excite us and capture our imaginations (189). Ashe suggests King Arthur's popularity in the United States may be based in Americans' tendency to speak about their "roots." But then he comments, "I doubt if this is the whole answer, since most Americans are not British descended" (189).

Actually, estimates of Americans of British (English, Irish, Scottish, and Welsh) descent run from 50-80% depending on the study. The number of studies and results on the Internet of how many Americans have British ancestry is too many to detail, but they can easily be found. Even people who identify themselves as African American often have Caucasian blood—and those descended from slaves with white blood will generally find that the Southern white slave owner in the family tree was of British descent. If we consider that King Arthur likely lived about the year 500 A.D. and we then consider how many descendants he had and how they migrated across the globe over fifteen hundred years, it is not much of a stretch to suggest that nearly everyone on earth can potentially be a descendant of King Arthur—provided he lived and did have children. DNA analysis recently has proven that everyone of European descent alive today can claim descent from anyone who lived in Europe prior to the year 1200 A.D.

In fact, as Steve Olson demonstrates in *Mapping Human History: Discovering the Past Through Our Genes,* if we go back just ten generations, we each would have 1024 ancestors, so thirty generations ago that number would be 1024 x 1024 x 1024, which equals over one billion. Since that many people did not live in the world thirty generations ago—estimates for the year 1400 were 375 million—many of our ancestors repeat, meaning our ancestors married distant cousins and shared similar ancestors. In any case, we can probably all claim descent from such famous ancient people as Confucius, Queen Nefertiti, and Julius Caesar (Olson 46-47). Furthermore, even people today of predominantly Asian or African descent could be descended from King Arthur. African-American poet Elizabeth Alexander, for example, is a descendant of King John of England (reigned 1199-1216 A.D.), as recently revealed on the PBS show *Faces of America with Henry Louis Gates, Jr.* broadcast in 2010. As Steve Olsen notes, "suppose an emissary from Ethiopia married a woman in the court of Henry II and had children. Today, all Europeans are descended from that Ethiopian" (46).

Anyone interested in genealogy knows that "race" does not really exist. In researching my own ancestry, I have found myself descended not only from people in every country in Europe but even China, India, and Persia. The human race is itself a melting pot. With these statistics, based in fact, not merely fancy, if King Arthur were a historical person, he is very likely ancestor to all of us. Our descent from King Arthur is obviously through his children, so we should learn more about them.

My own interest in King Arthur began when I first read *The Boy's King Arthur* at the age of fourteen. At twenty-one, I also began to take an interest in genealogy and traced my family back to King Edward III of England, among whose ancestors, of course, was Cerdic, King of Wessex, credited with being one of Arthur's greatest enemies. Imagine my surprise and interest when I read Geoffrey Ashe's suggestion that Cerdic was a possible son of King Arthur (199). If this relationship were true, then I would be a direct descendant of King Arthur! Something of a boyish pride swelled up in my heart, something that perhaps non-genealogists or non-lovers of Arthurian literature would not understand, but who would not like to claim descent from King Arthur? Later, I will discuss whether or not Cerdic is a possible son of King Arthur, but Geoffrey Ashe's suggestion was enough to spark my interest, especially when I learned King Arthur also had other children. The descendants of these other children must have multiplied so that by the 1600s, when Americans' British ancestors began journeying to the New World, several of them may have been carrying Arthurian blood over the seas with them. Not only I but thousands if not millions of other Americans would therefore be descendants of King Arthur!

If there were a King Arthur, then his descendants are probably more numerous than can ever be thoroughly traced. We may never know whether Arthur's descendants are living among us (or are us), as we may never know whether Arthur was a real person. However, both are pleasant thoughts, and I personally believe both may be more than just possibilities.

Even if it is not through blood, then through culture Americans are the descendants of Arthur and his times. The popularity of Arthurian literature can quickly transport anyone who reads a book or watches a film back to the Arthurian age. The ideals with which we credit Arthurian times, whether the period received those ideals from our time, or our time from the past, still serve to connect us.

Arthur's children are of interest to us, whether it is through genealogy or by cultural heritage. In *King Arthur's Daughter*, Vera Chapman makes this point nicely when she writes about the growth of Arthur's descendants:

> Not by a royal dynasty but by the spreading unknown and unnoticed, along the distaff line—mother to daughter, father to daughter, mother to son. Names and titles shall be lost, but the story and the spirit of Arthur shall not be lost. For Arthur is a spirit and Arthur is the land of Britain. (144)

Anyone who would be a descendant of King Arthur need not have a fifteen hundred-year-old pedigree to prove it; we need to tell the tales about Arthur, and when people hear these stories, he will then live on in their hearts and his line and descendants will continue to grow.

In the following pages, I will attempt to explore all the figures said to be descended from King Arthur, from the legend's earliest versions to the most modern novels. Often these modern novels are based on earlier traditions, or they are making their own interpretations of what could have happened. Arthurian studies always leave us the problem of trying to separate what is fact from fiction, and even the most respected Arthurian stories of the Middle Ages often become as suspect as the modern novels, and the modern novels today often try to be more authentic than their medieval counterparts; therefore, we must consider all interpretations and possibilities considering Arthur's children, whether they appear believable or not. In many cases, we will discover that what might have happened if Arthur were a historical person is not as important as how people have chosen to interpret or even rewrite Arthurian literature.

This book represents the first time King Arthur's children will all be assembled together, along with the various tales about them, as the subject of study. After looking more closely at the children of King Arthur, we will come to a better understanding of the purpose Arthurian literature has served over the centuries and perhaps we will even become more closely connected to King Arthur and his times.

Part I:
The Earliest Children in the Welsh Legends

Before Mordred made his appearance in the Matter of Britain and began to dominate it as the only son of King Arthur, just as he had tried to dominate Arthur's kingdom, the Welsh may have had the tradition that King Arthur had three sons. These three sons could be the earliest of Arthur's children to appear, but we have the least information about them, doubtless because much of it has been lost. Only one son, Llacheu, has any clear lines drawn as to where he may rightfully be integrated into the Arthurian legends. Another son, Amr, may have been the original of Mordred, while Gwydre's story comes down to us as faint as his ending is grim.

At times, scholars have either ignored or at least brushed these three sons aside as unimportant since no scholar has known what to think of them. Those scholars in the past who did not believe in a historical Arthur were more interested in studying the traditions and mythological background that went into forming the Matter of Britain. Since Arthur's three Welsh sons had such sketchy legends, little mythology survived for scholars to study the sons' origins. Furthermore, tradition says all three sons died before Arthur's passing, so none of them inherited his kingdom, and therefore, they have been considered of little importance. However, the belief in a historical King Arthur has continued to grow in recent years, and if there is any historical basis for his having had children, it seems only obvious, that if these are the earliest sons, they are the most likely to have existed in history. By closely exploring the traditions surrounding each of these sons, we may find a more solid place for them in Arthurian tradition.

Chapter 1: Gwydre

The only mention of Gwydre, the son of King Arthur, in any chronicle, appears in *The Mabinogion* tale of "Culhwch and Olwen." Arthur and his men are out hunting Twrch Trwyth, a prince who has been turned into a giant boar for his sins, because they need to obtain the comb between his ears as one of the tasks Culhwch must accomplish before Olwen's father will let him marry her. Arthur's men hold the boar at bay, which causes him to slay four of Arthur's champions, and "after he had slain those men, again he stood at bay against them there, and slew Gwydre son of Arthur" (Jones, *The Mabinogion*, 132). This passage is the only place in the tale that Gwydre, son of Arthur, is mentioned. He is not even listed earlier in the tale as being among Arthur's companions. When Gwydre dies, no mention is made of anyone weeping over his death, even though he is the son of a king; nor is there a story of his funeral. Norris J. Lacy and Geoffrey Ashe, judging from Gwydre's seeming insignificance, suggest that since neither Arthur nor anyone else seems to be upset over Gwydre's death, he was probably illegitimate (Lacy, *Arthurian Handbook*, 357).

Although nothing else is written about Gwydre in the Arthurian legends, Jennifer Westwood notes that Welsh tradition holds that the hunt for Twrch Trwyth took place in Powys, Wales where a monument stands to Arthur's sons who were killed in the hunt. This place is the Ty-newydd, also known as Cerrig Meibion Arthur, "The Stones of the Sons of Arthur" in the parish of Mynach log-Ddu, Dyfed (Westwood 338). Where this tradition of plural sons arises from is unknown. "Culhwch and Olwen" only mentions one son, so if more than one son was killed by Twrch Trwyth, those sons' names have disappeared into oblivion.

Even Gwydre's tale is so small that if more of it ever existed, it has long since been lost and forgotten. However, considering that Gwydre is a king's son, his story could have once been both significant and well-known. In many cases, certain Arthurian characters have been tracked back to mythological roots or stories that were cast onto them. Although no scholar has suggested it before, Gwydre may be such a case if we look at some characters from earlier Celtic myths and legends who have similar names and stories.

In his *Celtic Myth and Arthurian Romance*, R.S. Loomis compares the Celtic tale of Gwri to that of Mordred, and he states that the story was later cast onto Pope Gregory. Loomis describes Gwri's tale as one of illegitimate birth, which is exactly what Lacy and Ashe suggest for Gwydre. However, Loomis is only conjecturing about this illegitimate birth existing in a lost source since *The Mabinogion* version of the tale does not include an illegitimate birth. Loomis further describes Gwri's story as being one of exposure, fosterage by fishermen, enchainment on an island, and eventually deliverance from this imprisonment (335). This story does have obvious similarities with Mordred's tale, but perhaps we should also explore the idea that Gwydre's tale is based upon Gwri's.

One simple reason for believing that Gwydre and Gwri have a connection lies in the resemblance between their two names. One can easily see the spelling similarities between Gwri and Gwydre, and the connection becomes even more obvious when we learn that Gwri also had the name of Pryderi. If we conjecture that Gwri and Pryderi were combined to form a now forgotten name of Gwyderi, might it not be possible that the name was later condensed to Gwydre? The spelling similarity between Gwydre and Gwri is fairly obvious; however, if the tale comes from an oral tradition, we must look beyond the spelling to the pronunciation of the two names. If there had been the form of Gwyderi, could local dialect or rapid speech have caused the middle syllable to be omitted, leaving us with Gwydre? Perhaps Gwydre simply became confused with the character Gwri because their names sounded alike. Another possibility is that if the name of Gwydre were rapidly spoken, the "d" might not have been fully pronounced so that Gwydre would have sounded like Gwri to the undiscerning ear. We might even consider that Gwri is the earlier form of Gwydre because an intrusive "d" is not uncommon in English. Such possibilities would allow a closer connection between the two names, besides the similarity in their stories.

Gwri/Pryderi's tale is told in "Pwyll Prince of Dyfed" in *The Mabinogion*. Pwyll and his wife Rhiannon were without an heir to their kingdom. Pwyll's nobles urged him to take another wife. Pwyll said he would wait one more year, and if there were no heir by then, he would do as his nobles wished. Before the year was over, Rhiannon gave birth to a son. Six women sat up to watch over the mother and infant at night, but as morning approached, they all fell asleep. When the women awoke, the infant was gone. The women, in fear of being punished, concocted a terrible plot in which they killed the cub of a staghound, laid the bones by Rhiannon, and smeared her face and hands with blood. When Rhiannon awoke, the ladies told her that she had devoured her child in the night and overpowered all her women when they tried to stop her.

Despite Rhiannon's alleged crime, Pwyll still refused to have his wife put away. Instead, she was made to do penance every day by sitting at the gate of the castle, telling her tale to every stranger who came, and then carrying them on her back to the castle.

Meanwhile, Teirnyon of Gwent Is Coed had the most beautiful mare in the world, but although the mare foaled on the night of every 1st of May, no one ever knew what became of the colts. Teirnyon finally decided to find out what was happening, so he sat up on the night of the next colt's birth. As he was admiring the newborn's strength, he heard a great noise outside. Then a long, clawed arm came through the stable's window and laid hold of the colt. Teirnyon cut off the arm at the elbow with his sword so that it fell into the barn. He then heard a great wailing outside, but when he ran out of the barn, he could see nothing because of the night's darkness. He followed the noise for a short distance, but he finally returned to the stable where he found an infant, wrapped in swaddling clothes and a mantle of satin, lying by the door.

Teirnyon brought the infant to his wife, who was childless. She told her women she had given birth to it in the night, and so she adopted it as her own. The child was named Gwri of the Golden Hair, "for its hair was yellow as gold; and it grew so mightily that in two years it was as big and strong as a child of six" (Rolleston 364).

While the child was growing up, Teirnyon heard the tale of Rhiannon and noticed that Gwri resembled Prince Pwyll. Teirnyon then rode to the palace with the child. There he told the royal couple his story and how he suspected his foster son, Gwri, was really their child. Upon hearing this, Rhiannon cried, "I declare to heaven that if this be true there is an end to my trouble." Then a chief named Pendaran said, "Well hast thou named thy son Pryderi ('trouble') and well becomes him the name of Pryderi son of Pwyll, Lord of Annwn" (Rolleston 365).

Unlike Loomis' version of the tale, Pryderi/Gwri does not have an illegitimate birth in *The Mabinogion* version; however, the same tale of exposure seems to exist here, and in both cases, the child is raised by foster parents, although in *The Mabinogion* tale, they do not appear to be fishermen. The tale of Gwri may be the source for the lost tale of Gwydre; whether or not it definitely is, we cannot say, but for the moment, let us leave it open to possibility. We should also notice that in Gwri's tale, Rhiannon is barren at first, which must suggest to us the barren Guinevere. Secondly, we have another connection between Pryderi and Mordred; Tiernyon's baby colt disappears on the night of every May 1st. Although the text does not state the exact night that Pryderi was born, the night of his birth appears to be the same night that he was stolen. Doubtless, the creature who stole Pryderi was returning from his first theft via Tiernyon's home to steal the colt. Therefore, it can be assumed that Pryderi was born and stolen the same night the colt was born and stolen, on the night of May 1st, the same day that is the traditional birthdate of Mordred (Loomis, *Celtic Myth*, 339). Pryderi may then be a mythological ancestor to two of King Arthur's sons, both Gwydre and Mordred.

Now let us continue our comparison between Gwydre and Pryderi by looking at the tales of Pryderi's life as an adult. After the death of Pryderi's father, Pwyll, Pryderi's friend Manawyddan marries Pryderi's mother, Rhiannon. Pryderi and Manawyddan then make several failed attempts to gain their livelihood before they finally become hunters.

> One day they started a wild white boar, and chased him in vain until he led them up to a vast and lofty castle, all newly built in a place where they had never seen a building before. The boar ran into the castle, the dogs followed him, and Pryderi, against the counsel of Manawyddan, who knew there was magic afoot, went in to seek for the dogs.
>
> He found in the center of the court a marble fountain beside which stood a golden bowl on a marble slab, and being struck by the rich workmanship of the bowl, he laid hold of it to examine it, when he could neither withdraw his hand nor utter a single sound, but he remained there, transfixed and dumb, beside the fountain. (Rolleston 374)

Notice the similarities between Gwydre's hunting and being slain by a boar, and Pryderi's hunting of the boar. Pryderi is not slain by this boar, but it is the boar who leads him into the castle, the result of which is his touching the bowl and becoming like a statue; this state does not seem too dissimilar to death.

The tale continues with Manawyddan entering the castle, seeing what has happened, and returning home to tell Rhiannon. Being a mother, she rebukes Manawyddan for not stopping her son and his friend. The next day, Rhiannon visits the castle, and still seeing Pryderi clinging to the bowl, unable to move or speak, she also grabs hold of the bowl and joins him in his fate. Immediately afterwards is heard a peal of thunder and then a heavy mist falls. When the mist clears, the castle has vanished, along with Pryderi and Rhiannon.

The boar leading Pryderi into the castle has caused not only his immobility, but also his vanishing, which we might equate with death, thus saying that like Gwydre, Pryderi was killed by a boar.

However, Manawyddan accidently stumbles upon the cause of his friend and wife's disappearance, and through his cunning, Pryderi and Rhiannon are restored to him. Therefore, the boar really was not the end of Pryderi in this tale.

Pryderi ruled over one-and-twenty cantrevs of the south at the same time that Math was King of Gwynedd. King Math had two nephews, Gilvaethwy and Gwydion, and Math allowed them to run his kingdom while he "lay with his feet in the lap of the fairest maiden of the land and time, Goewin daughter of Pebin of Dol Pebin in Arvon" (Rolleston 378). Now Gilvaethwy fell in love with Goewin, and when he confided his love to his brother, Gwydion decided to help Gilvaethwy have his desire. Gwydion then went to Math and asked his leave to visit Pryderi and ask, as a gift for Math, for the herd of swine that Pryderi had received from Arawn, King of Annwn. Math gave his permission and Gwydion went to Pryderi's court. Pryderi, however, told Gwydion he was under a compact with his people neither to sell nor give the swine away until they had produced double their number in the land.

> "Thou mayest exchange them, though," said Gwydion, and thereupon he made by magic arts an illusion of twelve horses magnificently caparisoned, and twelve hounds, and gave them to Pryderi and made off with the swine as fast as possible. (Rolleston 379)

The intended result then happened—Pryderi invaded the land to regain his swine and Math went to meet him in battle, which gave Gilvaethy the opportunity to make Goewin his wife, although she was unwilling. The war was decided by single combat between Gwydion and Pryderi.

> And by force of strength and fierceness, and by the magic and charms of Gwydion, Pryderi was slain. And at Maen Tyriawc, above Melenryd, was he buried, and there is his grave. (Rolleston 379)

After the battle, Math returned home to discover what Gilvaethwy had done. Math took Goewin to be his queen, while

Gwydion and Gilvaethwy had to submit to Math for their punishment. Math then turned them into deer for a twelvemonth and told them to return at the end of that time. They returned with a young fawn, which was transformed into human shape and baptized. Then Math turned them into swine for a year, and again they came back with a young one who was treated as the fawn had been. The two brothers then underwent one more year of punishment as wolves, again returning with a young wolf. This time their penance was deemed complete, and they were returned to their human forms.

In this second tale of Pryderi, no boar hunt occurs, but there is a battle over swine, and since it resulted in his death, it could be said that the swine killed Pryderi. More striking, however, is that Gwydion, the murderer of Pryderi, as punishment for his crimes, was transformed into various animals, including a swine. This story almost perfectly resembles that of Gwydre, with the exception that his slayer, Twrch Trwyth, is a prince, son of King Taredd, who has already been transformed into a boar for his sins; here Gwydion is transformed after he commits murder because the transformation is his punishment for the murder.

Probably, the motif used in the case of Pryderi's murder is based on the classical or universal motif of a young man dying while still in his prime. In this case, if Pryderi's tale were used as a source for Gwydre's tale, obviously the same motif was used; however, the writer chose to be creative and reverse some elements of the motif so the killer of Gwydre is already a boar rather than someone turned into a boar after committing murder. No explanation is given of the sin the prince committed that led to his transformation into Twrch Trwyth, but it may not be too much of a stretch to assume that Gwydre and Twrch Trwyth's tale is the fragment of a larger tale that may go back to Pryderi and Gwydion.

One final point that must be made again connects Gwydre to Mordred. In almost every version of Mordred's story, he fights King Arthur in single combat, and the two end up slaying each other. Both Gwydre and Mordred are said to be King Arthur's sons, and if we accept Gwydre as being Pryderi, both are killed in single combat.

Rolleston, among others, has tried to make the connection that Arthur has a mythological source in Gwydion (349). However, although Gwydion and Arthur both slay someone, Pryderi is no relation to Gwydion, unlike the blood relation that usually exists between Arthur and Mordred. There seems to be little evidence to make a case for Arthur being some form of a solar god as Gwydion seems to be, so although the connection between Arthur and Gwydion is possible, it is not likely.

Gwydion and Pryderi's combat may be a tale that the Welsh writer of "Culhwch and Olwen" chose to adapt rather than use as a direct source for the tale of Gwydre since both Mordred and Gwydre would then be related to Arthur, with whom they do combat. Another possibility is that Gwydre never was Arthur's son until the writer of "Culhwch and Olwen" simply decided to attach this connection to him. One reason why the character of Gwydre could have been connected with Arthur may lie in another Gwydre mentioned in "Culhwch and Olwen" in the list of Arthur's companions. This Gwydre is not Arthur's son, but rather "Gwydre son of Llwydeu by Gwenabwy daughter of Caw, his mother (Hueil his uncle stabbed him, and thereby there was feud between Hueil and Arthur because of the wound)" (Jones, *Mabinogion*, 103). The recorder of the "Culhwch and Olwen" tale may have made the connection between Gwydre being stabbed by his uncle, Hueil, and Arthur and his nephew, Mordred, fighting each other. Perhaps the writer thought it would be clever to make this Gwydre Arthur's son and have him killed by a boar. The author, however, was not consistent in then changing the tale of the earlier Gwydre, son of Llwydeu.

The creation of a son of Arthur who is killed by a boar could be significant if the boar were meant to represent Arthur. King Arthur is often referred to as "The Boar of Cornwall," so could it not be said that Mordred, like Gwydre and Pryderi, was slain by a boar? Is Mordred's story then a later version of Gwydre's, which itself goes back to Pryderi? Or is it possible that the writer of "Culhwch and Olwen" knew nothing of Pryderi's tale, and simply borrowed Gwydre whose name already existed in "Culhwch and Olwen"? If such is the case, since *The Mabinogion* as we now have it was not written down until the late fourteenth century, then Mordred's tale could be older than Gwydre's rather than vice versa.

Geoffrey of Monmouth is our first known written source for Arthur being called the Boar of Cornwall. Where Geoffrey came up with this name for Arthur is unknown. Perhaps it existed in oral Welsh tradition, which is where Geoffrey may have derived it; it did not come from any written Welsh source that is extant today; in fact, *The Mabinogion* form of "Culhwch and Olwen" as we now have it is probably not the original Welsh story. Since *The Mabinogion* tales were not written down until the late fourteenth century, the scribes who recorded them could have been familiar with Geoffrey of Monmouth's work, and they might have even allowed it to influence them when for the first time, the oral Welsh tales were committed to paper. Consequently, a clever scribe, who knew that Arthur slew Mordred and that Arthur was often called the Boar of Cornwall, may have taken the character of Gwydre, who was killed by a boar, and decided to turn him into Arthur's son. Gwydre may have been chosen over the other characters slain by boars to be Arthur's son because he already had an existing Welsh story of being in conflict with his uncle. If such were the case, then perhaps Gwydre had no earlier story as Arthur's son that would link him to the character of Gwr/Pryderi. Mordred, as we will see in Part II, also may have not been Arthur's son, or even any relation to Arthur. He may have originally been simply a name in the legends whom writers adopted to be Arthur's son. The same may have been true for Gwydre. The possibility therefore exists that rather than Gwydre being a son of Arthur with an earlier story than Mordred, Mordred's tale could have influenced the creation of Gwydre as Arthur's son. Of course, it is possible that Gwydre also developed as a character, independent of Mordred, but considering Mordred's popularity, it seems more likely that Mordred influenced the creation of his reputed brother. However, we cannot decide with any certainty which son influenced the other's tale.

Another possibility, which does not have to concern Geoffrey of Monmouth, is that the writer of "Culhwch and Olwen" knew of

Nennius' story of Amr as a son of Arthur slain by his father (see Chapter 2), and at the same time a Welsh tradition existed of Arthur as the Boar of Cornwall. This information might inspire the writer to create Gwydre as Arthur's son, playing off Nennius' statement that Arthur slew his own son, while using the symbolism of the boar representing Arthur. It is possible, then, that the writer of "Culhwch and Olwen" developed the tale without any influence from Geoffrey of Monmouth, which would lead to the conclusion that Amr influenced the creation of Gwydre, and then both Amr and Gwydre were merged to help form the character of Mordred. Still, we have no proof of an existing Welsh tradition that calls Arthur the Boar of Cornwall, so it is probably unlikely to see Gwydre as having been created without some sort of influence from Geoffrey of Monmouth.

Other tales of heroes slain by boars and ladies abducted from their spouses or lovers may equally have influenced Gwydre's tale. The most notable tale in Celtic literature is that of Diarmuid and Grainne, which will be discussed in Chapter 3. The Welsh of this time period were also familiar with classical tales, so they may have borrowed the tale of Adonis being slain by a boar as a source for Gwydre's story. The Celtic tales may have been influenced by classical motifs, or they may simply employ universal motifs derived from one original prehistoric tale. It is beyond the reach of modern scholars to discover what the original sources of all these tales could have been. Of course, an obvious source for Gwydre's tale could be that people were commonly killed by boars during the Middle Ages in Wales, so the writer of "Culhwch and Olwen" was simply drawing upon the life he knew, and then he exaggerated it to turn a realistic event into a fascinating story.

Whether Gwydre was actually King Arthur's son or merely the creation of some writer, who could have been influenced by any number of sources, his being Arthur's son may have far more significance in "Culhwch and Olwen" than any scholar until now has pointed out. Whatever the evidence may show, he probably has some connection to Mordred, whether as a source or a result of Arthur's best known son.

Chapter 2: Amr

Amr is another of Arthur's early sons who appears in *The Mabinogion* with hardly anything mentioned about him. We are simply told in "Gereint Son of Erbin" that one of the four "chamberlains who guarded his (Arthur's) bed, none other than four squires" (Jones, *Mabinogion*, 231) was Amhar son of Arthur. Mention is not even made in *The Mabinogion* of who Amhar's mother was or whether he outlived his father.

Nennius is an even earlier source for this mysterious son of Arthur. In the *Historia Brittonum* or *The Marvels of Britain* (circa 800), Nennius states that Arthur killed his own son Anir (Fletcher 16-7), but no explanation is given as to why. Occasionally, Amr's name is also spelled as Amhar, and Lacy and Ashe are doubtless correct in assuming that Amhar and Amr are the same person (Lacy, *Arthurian Handbook*, 298). Another occasional spelling of the name is Amir.

Geoffrey of Monmouth also mentions Amr. He tells us that Amr is said to be buried at the Mt. of Ambrii, which may mean the Mt. of Ambrosii, or Ambrosius. Nennius also calls Ambrosius "Amir the Great," and Norma Lorre Goodrich points out that the other spelling of Amr's name as Amhyr comes from the Welsh version of his name which is Emrys and means Aurelius the Immortal (Goodrich, *King Arthur*, 55). Since the name is a form of Ambrosius, a Greek name meaning immortal, no one should be surprised since in most of the legends, Aurelius Ambrosius was King Arthur's uncle. Occasionally, Ambrosius is even said to be Uther's father, which would make him Arthur's grandfather; in any case, it has always been common for family names to be handed down from one generation to another.

Lacy and Ashe, as was the case with Gwydre, suggest that because of Amr's unimportance in the legends, he may have been Arthur's illegitimate child (Lacy, *Arthurian Handbook*, 298). However, before we accept this theory, we must ask why Amr's story is so vague. A son being slain by a boar is one thing, but a son killed by his own father is certainly a tale to make storytellers' imaginations run wild, so why did Amr become little more than a footnote in Arthurian literature?

Geoffrey Ashe suggests that the Welsh may have wished to suppress the fact that Arthur even had a son named Amr (196). He notes a tradition that Guinevere was King Arthur's second wife, as suggested by Gerald of Wales who saw the cross, discovered at Glastonbury Abbey along with Arthur and Guinevere's graves, that stated Guinevere was King Arthur's second wife (196). Ashe suggests that Arthur may have had a son, Amr, by his first wife, but the Welsh may have chosen to suppress this first wife, and consequently, the first wife's child (196).

Even if Arthur did have a first wife whom the Welsh chose to suppress, we need to ask why they wished to suppress her. Perhaps this "first wife" was actually a mistress or concubine of Arthur's. In this case, it is possible that retellers of the story may have thought it immoral, but it is doubtful that these retellers were the Welsh. Concubinage was an acceptable condition for the Welsh at this time. When Christian writers began recording the Arthurian legends, however, they may have twisted the Welsh tradition that Arthur had a concubine. Instead they changed the woman, who may have been the mother of Amr, from a concubine into Arthur's first wife. Even more than their desire to suppress the fact that Arthur, whom they saw as a Christian king, had a concubine, the Christian writers would have wanted to cover up the fact that Arthur could have had a child by this woman, a child whom the Church would have considered illegitimate. Therefore, such suppression was probably more likely to have come from Christian writers wishing to clean up an immoral plot, than the Welsh who freely accepted concubinage in their society.

Obviously, Amr's story brings to mind the conflict between Arthur and Mordred. We will probably never know what Amr did to upset his father, but it is doubtful Amr would have attempted to marry the queen if she were his own mother. We can then assume that if Amr is a source for Mordred, Amr is not the son of Guinevere.

Whether or not Arthur had mistresses or more than one wife, the tradition is that he slept with his half-sister, the result of course being that Mordred was conceived. We cannot know why the Welsh would suppress a first wife, but it seems reasonable that they would wish to suppress the fact that their hero, King Arthur, committed the sin of incest. It is Mordred, the son of this incest, whom Arthur slays. Mordred is charged with usurping his father's throne and trying to steal Guinevere. Could Amr have been guilty of the same acts?

Amr is the earliest written story of Arthur slaying his own son. Of course, there could have been older oral stories; however, the names of Arthur and Mordred do not appear together in writing until the tenth century in the *Annales Cambriae* which states that the two of them fell at Camlann together. Nennius seems to pre-date the *Annales Cambriae*, so unless Mordred was a character in oral tradition, Amr may be the older of the two characters in the Arthurian legends. Even when Mordred becomes known as Arthur's definite opponent at Camlann, such as in Geoffrey of Monmouth, he is merely Arthur's nephew, and only later did romancers transform him into Arthur's son. Amr is always stated to be Arthur's son.

Many scholars believe Mordred's incestuous birth is merely a motif affixed to the original story, something we will explore later in Part II; however, it is possible that Arthur did originally have a son by incest whom he slew, and whom the Christian recorders of the legend then tried to cover up; when the tale eventually leaked out, the origin of this forgotten son may have then been merged into the developing character of Mordred. Amr could then be a possible source for Mordred as the son of King Arthur, just as may be the case with Gwydre and Mordred.

However, before we become too confident in these assumptions, we must recall that Nennius says Amr's tomb is in Ercing (which is today in Hereford). This tomb is beside a stream called "the source of Anir." Nennius states that Anir is the man buried there, and he says, "He was the son of Arthur the warrior, who himself killed him there and buried him" (Fletcher 16-7).

Generally, the Battle of Camlann is believed to have taken place either at Hadrian's Wall or else in Cornwall. Hereford is a great distance both from Cornwall and Hadrian's Wall, so unless we wish to add Hereford to our list of possible sites for the Battle of Camlann, we have another dilemma.

One thing that does connect Cornwall to Amr's tomb in Hereford is pointed out by Jennifer Westwood. In Cornwall, on Craddock Moor, near Minions, are three stone circles of thirteen, seventeen, and nine surviving stones which go by the name of "The Hurlers." These stones were erected in the Stone Age for purposes unknown, but tradition says "they had beene men sometime transformed into stones, for profaning the Lords Day, with hurling" (25). (Hurling is a type of ball game native to Ireland and Cornwall.)

What connects the Hurlers to Amr's Tomb is that in 1675, Dr. James Yonge, a Plymouth surgeon, wrote that "they are now easily numbered, but the people have a story that they never could, till a man took many penny loaffes, and laying one on each hurler, did compute by the remainder what number they were" (Westwood 26). The tradition of countless stones is attached to several megalithic sites in Britain, including Stonehenge and Stanton Drew. Jennifer Westwood believes it is probably connected with the superstition attached by Nennius to Amr's Tomb, of which Nennius writes:

> and men come to measure the tumulus, sometimes six feet in length, sometimes nine, sometimes twelve, sometimes fifteen. In what measure you should measure it in its turn, the second time you will not find it in the same measure, and I have tested it myself. (Westwood 25-6)

Whether a connection exists between the strange behaviors of these various megalithic monuments and the story of Amr, we should remember that Nennius states Anir is buried at Mt. Ambrii, a name which may be a form of Aurelius or Ambrosius. Aurelius Ambrosius is always said to be buried at Stonehenge, and Stonehenge also has the strange tradition of it being impossible to count its many stones. Since Amr and Aurelius have similar names, were related, were both buried at megalithic monuments, and both have strange traditions attached to them, we cannot help but wonder whether they are the same person.

One possibility is that Geoffrey of Monmouth, familiar with Nennius' work, decided to borrow the son of Arthur buried at Mt. Ambrii and turn him into Aurelius Ambrosius. Geoffrey then decided to relocate him at Stonehenge since it was a more prominent and well-known monument than Mt. Ambrii. By making these alterations, Geoffrey had eliminated Amr as Arthur's son; he was then able to take Amr's character and tale and transfer them to Mordred. It is strange, however, that he does not make Mordred Arthur's son, but merely his nephew. Since Geoffrey may have been familiar with the statement in the *Annales Cambriae* that Arthur and Mordred had both died at Camlann, perhaps he felt his story would be more interesting if Mordred and Arthur killed each other, rather than Arthur killing his son and then outliving him. Geoffrey, therefore, decided to make Arthur's tale a definite tragedy. He was the first writer to do so.

If a connection exists between Mordred and any of the children who appear in the Welsh tradition, Amr seems to be the strongest link, and perhaps he is even the historical person who became the basis for the literary Mordred.

Chapter 3: Llacheu

We now come to a son of King Arthur, who like Gwydre and Amr, appears first in the Old Welsh tales, but for whom we have far more information.

Llacheu's first appearance is in a tenth-century poem in *The Black Book of Carmarthen*, which merely provides some obscure mentions of his death as only one of a number of dead heroes (Bruce, "Arthuriana," 179-80); his name also appears in "The Dream of Rhonabwy" in *The Mabinogion* as the son of Arthur. In one of the Triads, he is enumerated among the king's counsellors and called one of the three deivniawc of the isle of Prydein; deivniawc are "probablement inventeurs qui devinent la nature des choses" (Bruce "Arthuriana" 180). This label suggests he was a person who always looked beyond the surface, for truth and deeper meanings. He may not have been a sorcerer exactly but perhaps something closer to a seer. However, the increasing popularity of Merlin left no need for a lesser sorcerer, so this part of Llacheu's character may have purposely been omitted from his later appearances in Arthurian literature.

Llacheu also appears in "Erec and Enide" (late twelfth century) as Arthur's son, and two of this tale's manuscripts give his name as Lohous. Hartmann reproduced it as Lohut, and in *Perlesvaus* (first decade of the thirteenth century), it is Lohout in translation, but Loüt in the text, which is an emendation of the manuscript reading of Lont and Lant, both probably derived from Llacheu. Finally, in Wolfram von Eschenbach's *Parzival* and *Titurel* (both early thirteenth century), the character Ilinot is identical to Lohot, or Llacheu (Bruce, "Arthuriana," 179-81).

Llacheu is the only one, then, of King Arthur's sons who both originated in the Welsh stories and survived into the European chronicles. He may have once been a fairly prominent character, as Gwydre and Amr may have been, but then he faded out of the tales during the Middle Ages. Lacy and Ashe suggest that Llacheu may have been Arthur's illegitimate son (Lacy, *Arthurian Handbook*, 368); they seem overly fond of illegitimacy as a solution for mention of Arthur's lesser known children, but in Llacheu's case, they may be correct.

The first mention of Llacheu in the French Romances appears in line 1732 of Chretien de Troyes' twelfth-century *Erec*, where he is mentioned among the heroes as "Loholze li fiz le roi Artu." He next occurs in Ulrich von Zatzikhoven's *Lanzelet* in the late twelfth century. Here he is the son of both Arthur and Guinevere. His third appearance is in the French romances. The *Prose Lancelot* (about 1250) mentions him as one of the knights imprisoned in Dolorous Garde (Bruce, "Arthuriana," 181). He also appears most significantly in *Perlesvaus*. Finally, he is mentioned in Sir Thomas Malory where his name has been radically changed to Borre (Lacy, *Arthurian Handbook*, 368).

There are two major questions, just like in the cases of Amr and Gwydre, we must deal with when discussing the legends that have grown up around Llacheu; first, who is his mother, and second, how did he die?

In the earliest Welsh tradition, the name of Llacheu's mother does not appear. If Welsh tradition ever existed for his mother, it most likely made Llacheu the son of Guinevere. When the French discovered Llacheu, they made him the son of Arthur either by Guinevere or by a Lisanor, depending on whichever woman the writer chose (Bruce, "Arthuriana," 182).

The *Prose Lancelot* states that Llacheu the son of Lisanor of Cardigan had been seized by Brandus of the Isles and was being held prisoner inside Dolorous Garde (Goodrich, *Guinevere*, 76). In the *Livre d'Artus* (thirteenth century), believed to have been largely based on the *Prose Lancelot*, Arthur, upon Merlin's advice, makes the acquaintance of Lisanor, daughter of Sevan, lord of the castle of

Canparcorentin. She comes to pay homage to Arthur, and he begets on her a son. In *Le Livre de Lancelot del Lac* is another story of Arthur being imprisoned by the beautiful sorceress Camille. Through her magic, Arthur falls madly in love with her, and she seduces him. Arthur is eventually rescued by Guinevere and Lancelot, but before the rescue happens, it is possible he made Camille pregnant with his child (Goodrich, *Guinevere*, 60). The last appearance of Llacheu is in Malory, where it again states that Arthur had a son by Lyonors; although this son is named Borre, we can assume it is the same story as that of Llacheu born by Lisanor (Lacy, *Arthurian Handbook*, 368).

However, both in *Lanzelet* and *Perlesvaus*, Llacheu is the legitimate son of Arthur and Guinevere; that he is depicted as Guinevere's son allows him to play more important roles in these two works.

In Ulrich von Zatzikhoven's *Lanzelet*, Llacheu (here spelled Loüt) makes a brief but important appearance. Guinevere is being held captive in a castle by King Valeran. Lancelot and some other knights are trying to decide how to rescue her when Llacheu arrives; naturally, he wishes to aid in the rescue of his mother (*Lanzelet* 119). A council is held to decide what should be done, and of course, Lancelot, being the hero of the work, is chosen to do the actual rescuing. We are not even told whether Llacheu said anything at the council meeting or played any actual role in the rescue; he is never mentioned again in the work.

However, Llacheu makes a grand appearance for the short time he is on the scene, since the author writes of him,

> We have seldom heard in any kind of story that there
> was ever a knight more courtly...never did any young man
> win more renown than Loüt from the time that he began to
> bear a sword until he rode away, as the tale tells us, with
> Arthur, his noble father, into a country whence the Bretons
> still expect both of them evermore. (Lanzelet 119)

One would wonder, since Llacheu is so obscure, whether the author is just making up nice things to say about him, but in the

notes to her edition of *The Mabinogion*, Lady Charlotte Guest
points out that Llacheu is described in one of the Welsh Triads.

> Llacheu is mentioned with Gwalchmai and Rhiwallon of
> the broom blossom hair, as one of the learned ones of the
> Island of Britain to whom the elements and material
> essence of every thing were known. He was no less
> renowned for warlike prowess than for his deep
> knowledge, and is said to have fallen fighting bravely for
> his country, in the battle of Llongborth, so celebrated in
> the verse of Llywarch Itên. (Guest, *Mabinogion*, 351)

The Welsh tales and Ulrich von Zatzikhoven are in agreement
then about the noble character and greatness of Llacheu; if they are
able to rave about Llacheu, then he may have figured prominently in
earlier traditions or stories, now lost to us. However, what these
two sources are not in agreement about is Llacheu's end.

Ulrich gives us the surprising statement that Llacheu rode off
with his father, King Arthur, and like his father, he will someday
return. This work is the first surviving one to make such a
statement, and it was probably invented by Ulrich, unless he got it
from one of his unknown French sources (Bruce, "Arthuriana,"
181). This belief did not end with Ulrich, however, for we will find
in the modern Arthurian fiction that writers have invented tales of
children of King Arthur returning, and even that these children, like
their father, will be saviors of Britain.

The Welsh tradition, however, is clear in stating that Llacheu
died at the Battle of Llongborth. Lady Charlotte Guest further
points out that Llacheu's death is alluded to in a curious dialogue
between Gwyn ab Nudd and Gwyddno Garanhir. Rhys gives both
the original Welsh and his translation:

> Mi awum lle llas llachev
> mab arthur uthir ig certev.
> ban ryreint brein ar crev.
>
> I was there where lLacheu fell,

> Arthur's son renowned in song,
> When ravens flocked on the gore. (Rhys 60)

The mention of the ravens in this passage further backs up the idea that Llacheu was slain in battle since in Celtic tradition, the Morgana, the goddess of death, would appear in the form of a raven flying over the battlefield.

Another source for Llacheu's death, not giving details as to how he died, is provided by Bleddyn Fardd, who states "Llachau was slain below Llech Ysgar." It is not known exactly where Llech Ysgar was, but it is known to have been one of Madog ap Maredudd's courts in Powys during the twelfth century (Bromwich, *Arthur of the Welsh*, 44).

The French, however, when they learned the Welsh tradition that Arthur had a son, either ignored or did not know his true place in the legends and simply let their imaginations run wild (Bruce, "Arthuriana," 184). It may be Geoffrey of Monmouth's responsibility that Arthur's sons disappeared from later versions of the legends; *The History of the Kings of Britain* was so popular that it firmly placed a structure on the way the tale would be told from then on, and since Geoffrey did not give Arthur any sons, his successors avoided creating sons for Arthur. And if writers had added sons to the legend, they would have had to come up with explanations for why these sons did not succeed their father. However, the fact that Llacheu does appear in romances written after Geoffrey of Monmouth is a clear indication that the French writers had some knowledge (however limited it may have been) of the Welsh traditions from Breton traditions, independent of Geoffrey of Monmouth (Bruce, "Arthuriana," 179).

One aspect of Llacheu's story the French appear to have added was his illegitimacy through his mother Lisanor, a woman who is probably completely fictional. More importantly, the French and their followers created a whole new death story for Llacheu that has come down to us in two different, but closely related versions.

In all of these versions, Llacheu is slain by Sir Kay. Several scholars have suggested that the source for Kay's murdering Llacheu was Llacheu and Kay's names being mentioned together in *The Black Book of Caermarthen* as follows:

> Unless it were God who accomplished it,
> Cai's death were unattainable.
> Cai the fair and Llachau,
> they performed battles
> before the pain of blue spears [ended the conflict].
>
>   (Bromwich, *Arthur of the Welsh*, 43)

The two warriors may have fallen together in battle, but Bruce and other scholars believe it is evident from the way the names are coupled that Kay was not Llacheu's slayer in Welsh tradition (Bruce, "Arthuriana," 184). Kay seems to have been accused of murdering Llacheu, much as the mention of Arthur and Mordred falling together at Camlann in the *Annales Cambriae* may have been interpreted as Mordred revolting against Arthur.

In his *Studies in the Arthurian Legend*, John Rhys gives one version of Llacheu's murder which he takes from the second part of the Welsh version of the Grail, the *Seint Greal*. In this version, Llacheu seeks adventure and fights a giant named Logrin, who has proven himself one of King Arthur's cruelest foes and allows no one to live in the same country with him. Llacheu succeeds in killing the giant and then lies down on the giant's body and falls asleep. Kay then rides up, discovers this strange sight, and beheads Llacheu and the giant. He then returns to court, claiming he slew the giant. The court makes much of him, but soon his treachery is known and hostility grows between Arthur and Kay, causing Kay to flee to his own castle (61).

Another version of this story occurs in the *Perlesvaus*, a French work of the early thirteenth century. Here everything occurs as in the last story up to where Kay kills Llacheu. This time, Kay cuts off both the giant and Llacheu's heads and brings Llacheu's body, along with the giant's head, back to court, claiming he killed the giant who had killed Llacheu. Later a damsel comes to court with a coffer containing Llacheu's head, and she tells the story of his death. Guinevere recognizes the head as having belonged to her son from a scar that is on it; the sight of it causes her to die of grief (Bruce, "Arthuriana," 182).

Caitlin and John Matthews, in the *The Arthurian Book of Days* (1990), give a version of the tale that makes Kay look more like a victim than a murderer; however, they do not give their source. It appears in the entry for March 15, as follows:

> Arthur sat in solemn justice to hear the defence of his foster brother. Kay stammered his sorry tale: "Upon my last quest I encountered a giant who made me play a beheading game. I knew the way of it, I thought, since Gawain's contest those many Christmases ago. Instead of himself, the giant sent forth against me a knight who acquitted himself nobly, but I overcame him and struck off his head. It was not till the helmet was off that I saw it was Loholt, and that I had been tricked into treachery. Until the ending of my life, I repent that stroke." (45-6)

Here Morgain interrupts to relate that the giant is the brother of King Arthur's enemy, King Rhitta, and that this event is the sorrow she foretold.

> And since Kay had been shamed by such a trick, Arthur forgave him before all, though Guinevere was less forgiving. (45-6)

Since Caitlin and John Matthews do not give a source for this version of Llachue's death, it seems logical to assume that they were merely rewriting the tale as it appeared in the *Perlesvaus* since Kay's motive for murdering Llacheu is not expressed in that work; furthermore, they also added in the detail of Gawain playing a beheading game, an event that occurs in *Sir Gawain and the Green Knight*, a late fourteenth century Middle English work; the Matthewses reinterpret the tale by giving Kay a form of motivation for killing Llacheu, which makes Llacheu's murder more plausible.

In the two earlier versions, Kay is clearly an intended murderer, rather than a victim of someone else's evil deeds. This depiction of Kay is surprising since in the Welsh tales he usually appears as the greatest, or at least one of the greatest of Arthur's warriors, plus his loyal subject, friend, and foster-brother. However, Kay is sometimes depicted as being touchy toward Arthur as at the end of "Culwch and Olwen," where a hint of some discord between Arthur and Kay exists, although it seems unlikely that in the Welsh tradition Kay would have stooped to murdering Arthur's son; therefore, the story of Llacheu's murder is probably of continental origin.

Rhys suggests that Kay was not only like Lancelot in being Arthur's greatest warrior in certain legends, but a lost tradition may have existed of Kay being Guinevere's lover. Rhys bases this theory on a Welsh dialogue between Guinevere and Arthur taken from the *Myvyrian Archeology.*

Arthur.

Du yw fy march a da dana',
Ac er dwr nid arswyda,
A rhag ungwr ni chilia.
Black is my steed and brave beneath me,
No water will make him fear,
And no man will make him swerve.

Gwenhyvar.

Glas yw fy march o liw dail,
lLwyr dirmygid mefl mawrair:
Nid gwr ond a gywiro ei air
Green is my steed of the tint of the leaves
No disgrace like his who boasts and fails:
He is no man who fulfills not his word.

Arthur's next triplet has been lost, along with the beginning of Gwenhwyvar's answer.

..... ymlaen y drin
Ni deil gwr ond Cai hir ab Sefin.
..... in the forefront of the fray
No man holds out but Kei the Tall, son of Sevin.

Arthur.

Myfi a ferchyg ac a sai',
Ac a gerdda yn drwm gan lan trai:
Myfi yw'r gwr a ddaliai Gai.
It is I that will ride and will stand,
And walk heavily on the brink of the ebb:
I am the man to hold out against Kei.

Gwenhyvar.

Dyd was rhyfed yw dy glywed:
Onid wyd amgen no'th weled
Ni dalid di Gai ar dy ganfed.
Pshaw, young man, it is strange to hear thee!
Unless thou be other than thou lookest,
Thou wouldst not, one of a hundred, hold against Kei.

Arthur.

Gwenhwyfar olwg eirian
Na difrawd fi cyd bwy; bychan
Mi a daliwn gant fy hunan.
Gwenhwyvar of the bright face,
Do not insult me small though I be:
I would hold against a hundred myself.

Gwenhwyvar.

Dyd was o du a melyn,
Wrth hir edrych dy dremyn
Tybiais dy weled cyn hyn.
Pshaw, young man of black and yellow!
After scanning long thy looks
Methought I had seen thee before.

Arthur.

Gwenhwyfar olwg wrthroch,
Doedwch i mi, os gwydoch,
Y'mha le cyn hyn i'm gwelsoch.

Gwenhwyvar of the—face,
Tell me if you know it,
Where you saw me before.

> Gwenhwyvar.

Mi a welais wr gradol o faint
Ar fwrd hir Arthur yn Dyfnaint
Yn rhannu gwin i'w geraint.
I have seen a man of moderate size
At Arthur's long table in Devon,
Dealing out wine to his friends.

> Arthur.

Gwenhwyfar barabl digri',
Gnawd o ben gwraig air gwegi:
Yno y gwelaist di fi.
Gwenhwyvar of facetious speech,
It is woman's nature to banter:
There it is thou didst me see.

Rhys suspects that this dialogue hints at Kay being Guinevere's original ravisher, and that she was in no hurry to leave him. He furthermore believes that such a tale would be in agreement with the story of Kay's having murdered Llacheu (59). Perhaps this dialogue hints at the origins of what later became the Lancelot story. Although Lancelot is not guilty of slaying Arthur's son, he does slay Arthur's nephew Gareth. Furthermore, he also abducts or rescues the queen, flees to his own castle, and makes war on Arthur. What does not fit is that Guinevere would praise Kay if he were the murderer of her son. Kay's actions make him suspiciously look like he plans to usurp the throne by murdering the heir and then following the old matriarchal tradition that he who has the queen rules the land. Furthermore, because Kay was Arthur's foster-brother, he may have believed that Arthur would pass the throne on to him, and in some versions of the legend, Kay is even said to be a relative of Arthur, which may mean they had closer ties than as foster-brothers; such a blood relationship might make the possibility of kingship a reality for Kay.

Still, Rhys' suggestion that these lines refer to Kay as the ravisher of Guinevere may be overlooking a more obvious answer. It has always been common for people to belittle great warriors, so they will become angry and be more fierce warriors in battle. Guinevere could simply be doing the same here, but even so, it would be strange for her to mention Kay, rather than some enemy, as the one who will defeat Arthur. Even if Kay is not a ravisher of Guinevere, he appears to be fighting on the opposite side of Arthur.

Some scholars believe this contradiction in Kay's character is the result of a mythological story being imposed upon him. J.D. Bruce suggests it is barely possible that Kay's murdering of Llacheu may go back to Celtic myth (Bruce, "Arthuriana," 184). If a Welsh tradition existed that Kay abducted the queen, and no tradition that he murdered her son, then it would also make it more believable that Guinevere was in love with Kay. However, since no such tradition has survived, it is doubtful Kay and Guinevere ever were lovers.

Writing in 1891 as a disciple of the theoretical school of solar gods, Rhys believes the death of Llacheu may go back to a solar god tale. Rhys suggests that the name Llacheu must be related to the Welsh adjective *llachar* as meaning "gleaming, flashing." He interprets *llachee* as a common noun to mean gleams and flashes (61). Perhaps the name is also related to Lleu, the most remarkable of the Welsh sun-heroes, which became Lug or Lugh in Irish (97). We will come across this possibility again in Chapter 7.

Rhys then argues that Llacheu's habit of sleeping on his fallen foe's body goes back to a curious nature myth. His opponent represents the giant of darkness who fills the world with his ravages. When this giant is vanquished and slain, his carcass is identical with the vast body of the ocean where, according to Celtic legend, darkness takes refuge. Llacheu, representing light, by his lying on the giant's body, is covering darkness as the sun vanishes the dark. However, darkness again becomes victorious when the sun-god is killed, and in this legend, Kay kills Llacheu, making Kay the representative of darkness (61-2).

Rhys backs up his theory that Llacheu is the inheritor of a solar god myth by pointing out that Llacheu was said to have worn a circle of gold to distinguish him as a king's son. Rhys believes that Llacheu's circle of gold, taken with his marvellous knowledge of all material things and the meaning of his name, is proof that Llacheu's nature is as a solar person (61). However, Rhys does not give his source for this circle of gold that Llacheu wore, and I have not been able to find a source for it, so this statement could be his own conjecture, trying to impose his theory on the facts. It is not even clear what this circle of gold may be; possibly it is a torc, a type of Celtic necklace, but torcs were commonly worn among the Celtic peoples, so Llacheu's wearing one makes him no more of a solar god than anyone else in Arthurian literature.

Another possibility is that Rhys misread the *Perlesvaus*. Here Perceval obtains a circlet of gold and becomes known as the Knight of the Golden Circlet (Evans 213). Arthur, not yet aware that his son Llacheu (here named Lohot) has died, believes this unnamed knight is his son, but later Arthur finds out that Lohot was murdered by Kay and that the Knight of the Golden Circlet is really Perceval (Evans 233). In this case, the Golden Circlet is a type of crown, and it is referred to in one place as a "crown of thorns" (Evans 164); however, it is not worn by Lohot, so it does not strengthen Rhys' theory that Lohot is a solar god. Furthermore, the solar god school of theorists has fallen into disrepute since Rhys' time for its oversimplifications and the limits of the scholarship of the nineteenth century; we need to keep considering the possibilities for Llacheu as a historical son of Arthur, as well as possible mythical origins.

Llacheu, as a king's son, like his brothers Gwydre and Amr, must have a tomb. As mentioned already, Llacheu's death greatly upset Guinevere who could not forgive Kay for what he had done. The death of Llacheu, in *Perlesvaus*, is even attributed as causing Guinevere to die of grief (Lacy, *Arthurian Encyclopedia*, 424-5). The interest Guinevere shows in Llacheu's death must surely be maternal, which further strengthens the likelihood of his being Arthur's legitimate son rather than the child of the undoubtedly fictional Lisanor. Norma Goodrich even suggests that Llacheu was next in line for the throne; therefore, Llacheu's death must have occurred before Arthur left to do battle against the Romans on the continent, resulting in Arthur having to choose a new regent and heir before he left, the choice being his son/nephew, Mordred (Goodrich, *King Arthur*, 258, 262).

Soon after discovering Lohot has died in *Perlesvaus*, Guinevere dies of grief. Arthur then has Guinevere's body and Lohot's head buried together in Avalon where Guinevere had built a tomb for them when they died (Evans 281-2).

With all this information, scholars believe Llacheu was definitely a son of King Arthur who is not to be confused with either Gwydre or Amr. However, since both Gwydre and Amr have connections to Mordred, it is natural to question whether the same is true for Llacheu. Recall that in the *Perlesvaus* a damsel brought the slain Llacheu's head to the court and Guinevere recognized it as her son's head by a scar upon it. The tradition of being able to identify someone by a scar or birthmark is quite common in literature; Ulysses is identified by his nurse when he finally returns home in *The Odyssey* because of a scar on his knee. In the *Huth Merlin*, Mordred is said to have also had a scar he received from an accident with his cradle as a child (Bruce, "Arthuriana," 182). Could there be a connection here between Mordred and Llacheu?

The answer might be found in the old Irish myth of Diarmuid, where the hero has a scar from a magical boar, which also reminds us of Gwydre's death by a boar. In the Irish tale, Diarmuid meets Fionn, whose wife, Grainne, was stolen from him by Diarmuid, which immediately reminds us of Mordred stealing Guinevere from Arthur. Fionn tells Diarmuid that the wild boar of Gulban was being hunted, but as always, in vain. Diarmuid's father had killed Roc's son in the sid of Oengus, and Roc had transformed the body into a boar which would have the same length of life as Diarmuid; it was prophesied that by this boar, Diarmuid would fall. Oengus had placed his son under a *geiss* never to hunt a boar. Diarmuid, however, desired to slay the boar of Gulban, the transformed child, although he knew that he had been brought to it through Fionn's wiles. In the hunt that followed, "the old fierce magic boar" was killed, although not before it had mortally wounded the hero. In other versions, Diarmuid is unhurt, but Fionn bade him pace the boar to find out its length, and while doing so, a bristle entered Diarmuid's heel and made a deadly wound. As Diarmuid lay dying, Fionn taunted him. Diarmuid begged for water because whoever drank it from Fionn's hands would recover from any injury; Fionn brought water several times, but he let it trickle away before giving it to Diarmuid and so Diarmuid died (MacCulloch 177-8, MacCana 111).

In this story we have a scar, as Llacheu and Mordred both have. We have a man abducting another man's wife as is the case with Mordred abducting Guinevere. Finally, we have a boar, who is actually a human under enchantment, kill the hero just as the boar, formerly human, kills Gwydre. If this story connects Llacheu to Gwydre and to Mordred, and we have already seen connections between Gwydre, Amr, and Mordred, then does it not seem possible that all three of these Welsh sons were combined to form the character of Mordred? Arthur's children, the three most likely candidates for being historical, may well have been consolidated into one son used for dramatic purposes to turn the historical King Arthur into the man of legend.

Part II:
Mordred

Chapter 4: Mordred's Birth and Origins

We now arrive at Mordred, the best known, and most prominent of King Arthur's children. However, because so much information exists in the legends concerning Mordred, and consequently so much has been written about him by scholars, he is the most complicated of King Arthur's children to understand. In fact, we cannot even be sure that he is one of Arthur's children. He does appear in some of the legend's earliest versions, but unlike his would-be brothers, Gwydre, Amr, and Llacheu, there is no simple statement that he is Arthur's son. In fact, the first reference of his relationship to Arthur is not as his son but merely as his nephew. To determine who the real Mordred may have been, we have to separate him from the many legends and look at how his character changed in various literary depictions over the centuries. Our first question then must be how did Mordred originate? The answer may help us determine whether Mordred can actually qualify as a son of King Arthur.

Various theories have been put forth about the origin of Mordred's name, the Welsh form of which is Medraut or Medrawt. One theory is that the name is derived from the Welsh verb *medr-u*, meaning "to hit with a missile," or metaphorically to be hit with the sense of knowledge or understanding. This name may also have some connection or derivation from Medr or Medyr, a character in "Culhwch and Olwen" who could shoot an arrow from Cornwall that would evenly pass through the legs of a wren in Ireland (Rhys 38-9). If we prefer the more metaphorical meaning of the name, it may have some relation to the Irish word *midiur*, meaning "I judge." Rhys believes this connotation may connect Mordred to the Irish God, Midir, but modern scholars find this derivation unlikely

(37-8). The French romancers turned the name into Mordred, a name possibly connected with Mordrain, suggesting that the name's origins lie in the Welsh deity Medrod (Loomis, *Celtic Myth*, 149). This name change, we will discover in Chapter 5, may have had a major influence on the way Mordred's character was viewed. Rhys' remark on the origin of Mordred's name follows:

> whatever the origin of the name Medrawt or Medrod may be, the Breton and Cornish forms involve a difficulty which should have been noticed. The Cornish one appears early as Mordred (*Revue Celtique* i. 335) apparently under the influence of such English names as Aelfred and Aethelred. Otherwise it must have followed suit with the Old Breton form, which was Modrot. The Welsh forms Medrawt and Medrod point to an earlier stage, Mëdrot or Mëdrat; but Mëdrot will explain the Breton form too, if only we suppose its second vowel to have attracted its first to its own sound (392).

Moland suggests the romancers derived the form Mordred from the Latin *moror* and *credere*, and that it means "slow in belief" (Loomis, *Celtic Myth*, 146). However, Mordred's character has nothing that would make this meaning symbolic to him. Although unlikely, many modern writers, particularly those supporting New Pagan ideas, suggest that the name was derived from Mordrain or has some connection to Modron, a possible sister of Morgan le Fay or sometimes even a brother to Arthur. (For more information on Modron, see the appendix).

Given these theories, none of which is definite, the name of Mordred is probably of Welsh rather than Latin origin. Mordred definitely appears in the Welsh legends and histories, and although he does not become a major character until Geoffrey of Monmouth, he was not an invention of that writer.

The first mention of Mordred appears in the tenth century *Annales Cambriae* for the year 539, where it states that Arthur and Mordred both fell at Camlann. No mention is made of a relationship between Arthur and Mordred or even if they were on the same or opposing sides. Blaess observes that the first mention of King Arthur having any nephew occurs in William of Malmesbury's *Geste Regum Anglorum* written sometime before 1125; however, the nephew mentioned here is not even Mordred, but Walwin, an early version of Gawain (Blaess 69).

In *The History of the Kings of Britain*, which appeared about 1136, Geoffrey of Monmouth gave Arthur several nephews including Mordred, and from that time on, Mordred became a key figure in the Arthurian legends. Fletcher suggests that Mordred was developed as Arthur's nephew prior to Geoffrey of Monmouth, but no evidence survives to verify this assertion (81). Mordred does appear in the Welsh *Mabinogion* tale "The Dream of Rhonabwy" as King Arthur's nephew, here named as Medrawd (Jones, *Mabinogion*, 140; Guest, *Mabinogion*, 138). However, as we have already seen, these Welsh tales, although their origins may be older than Geoffrey of Monmouth's work, were not written down until the fourteenth century or later, so they could have been influenced by Geoffrey of Monmouth's writing, thus making them unreliable as the oldest sources for Arthurian characters or plots.

In Layamon, Mordred remains merely Arthur's nephew, the son of Arthur's sister and Walwain's brother (235). Not until such works as the Vulgate *Mort Artu* and the *Huth Merlin* does Mordred appear as King Arthur's son; in both of these works, Mordred is born because Arthur unknowingly commits incest with his half-sister, Morgause (Lacy, *Arthurian Encyclopedia*, 394; Bruce, *Evolution*, vol. 2, 319). Incest may be shocking to modern day readers, but the author of the *Mort Artu*, who seems responsible for introducing it into the legends around 1205, had good reason for adding this detail to the plot. The author probably felt that Mordred would be a more interesting traitor if he slew his own father. But from a moral standpoint, the author had to answer the question of why, if Arthur was such a good man and a good king, would God allow him to be murdered? Through making Mordred the child of incest, the author was showing how man is punished for his sins; therefore, because Arthur commits sin with his sister, even though he does it unknowingly, he is punished (Bruce, *Evolution*, vol. 1, 441).

While the author may have had his theological reasons for introducing incest into the legend, the incest-motif goes back to ancient literature. Incest tales already existed in Oedipus, the Bible, and the stories of Pope Gregory; an example of sibling incest is the character of Roland, who is said to be the son of Charlemagne and Charlemagne's sister (Bruce, *Evolution*, vol. 1, 441). These examples, however, may be distant from the original sources of incest in the Arthurian legend.

R.S. Loomis points out the abundance of incest tales in Celtic mythology, some of which closely correspond to Mordred's story. One such tale is that of Eochaid Bres, who was the offspring of Delbaeth's son and daughter, and who like Mordred, became the opponent of his father in swordplay (Loomis, *Celtic Myth*, 341). Another example lies in the riddle of the birth of Cuchulain which says Cuchulain's father was also his uncle (Cowan 99); the only way this relationship would be possible was if Cuchulain's parents were brother and sister.

The incest tale from Irish Celtic literature that may best fit Mordred's story is the tale of the Celtic god Dylan. Dylan was the son of Gwydion and Arianrhod, who were brother and sister (Rolleston 350, 381). After Gwydion and Arianrhod committed incest, Arianrhod gave birth to two sons, one of whom was named Dylan, meaning "Son of the Wave." As soon as Dylan was baptized, "he plunged into the sea and swam as well as the best fish that was therein....Beneath him no wave ever broke" (Rolleston 380). Later in the tale, Dylan was killed by his uncle Govannon, and when this happened, all the waves of Britain and Ireland wept for him so that the roar of the incoming tide at the mouth of the river Conway is still known as the "death-groan of Dylan" (Rolleston 380).

Like Mordred, Dylan is the child of incest, and he is killed by his uncle; even in those Arthurian versions where Arthur is Mordred's father, he is always Mordred's uncle since Mordred's mother is Arthur's sister. In most versions of the Arthurian legend, when Arthur discovers that his sister has given birth to the child of their incest, he fears the prophecy of Merlin that this child will cause his downfall. Arthur then orders all babies born at that time to be drowned. Mordred is thrown into the sea, but he survives and is washed ashore, where he is then found and raised by fisherfolk; this tale resembles that of Gwri, with the exception that Gwri was not thrown into the sea; Dylan was thrown into the sea and also slain by his uncle, so Dylan's tale may have an even closer correspondence to Mordred than Gwri's tale.

As already stated, Mordred may or may not have been developed as a character before Geoffrey of Monmouth; however, we know a tradition existed that Arthur had a son or sons earlier than the time of Geoffrey of Monmouth. These sons may have been the children of an earlier wife or mistress of Arthur, or possibly even the sons of Arthur's sister. If Mordred is based on one of these earlier sons, he seems most similar to Amr. If Mordred is a later version of Amr, and Amr had been thrown into the sea because he was the child of incest, he certainly would have had good reason for hating the father who had ordered him drowned.

The idea of incest between brother and sister may be repulsive to us today, but it was only in the twentieth century that the United States made it illegal to marry a relative closer than a third cousin; in foreign countries, particularly in the Middle East, it is still common for first cousins to marry one another. Originally, the Jewish laws forbade incest, a taboo later adopted by Christianity. Christianity's dominant influence over Western Europe has made incest repulsive to most readers of the Arthurian legend; however, in fifth century Britain, before Christianity had completely become the dominant religion in the British Isles, some cultures may have practiced incest and even saw it as desirable. Norma Goodrich points out Olrik's suggestion that such a tradition may be reflected in the Mordred birth story (*Guinevere* 48).

In this tradition, incest may have been practiced by Arthurian royalty for the purposes of genetic engineering. The family may have intended to preserve or even double certain traits such as intelligence, courage, beauty, and strength (Goodrich, *Guinevere*, 48). What may be even more important in the case of royalty would be the concept of keeping the money or the throne in the family. It has never been uncommon for royalty to marry their relatives; Queen Elizabeth II and Prince Philip are third cousins, and William III and Mary II were first cousins. The Middle Ages are filled with examples of royal or noble families in which uncles married their nieces. In fact, to marry one's near relative occasionally was even considered virtuous in the ancient world. In the late Zoroastrian work "The Vision of Arda Viraf," composed sometime between 226-641 A.D., a visionary learns that a person who wishes to achieve virtue can partially do so by contracting a next-of-kin marriage (Campbell 195); however, such societies were generally exceptions to the rule. Besides the Jewish and Christian societies, the Norse and the Greeks also frowned upon incest.

The theory that the incest in the Arthurian legends may have been committed for a purpose other than evil has been followed up by Marion Zimmer Bradley in her novel *The Mists of Avalon* (1982). Here, Vivian, the Lady of the Lake, engineers it so that Morgan and her half-brother, Arthur, unknowingly sleep together. Through the child born of their sexual relations, Arthur and Morgan more closely unite the two royal lines of Britain. Their child is descended through Arthur and Morgan's mother, Igraine, from the ancient royal British lines, while through Arthur's father, Uther, the child is descended from the royal blood of Rome.

If Mordred were developed as a character before Geoffrey of Monmouth, he may have been the son of King Arthur through Arthur's committing incest with his own sister. The Christian writers, who considered incest to be morally wrong, may have wished to hide the fact that Arthur, a Christian king, would have had an incestuous relationship. This cover-up could explain why Geoffrey of Monmouth and other writers portrayed Mordred simply as Arthur's nephew rather than his son. However, the truth of Mordred's incestuous birth, despite the Christian writers' efforts to hide it, may have still managed to leak out.

The author of the *Mort Artu* may have been the one fully to expose this story of incest around 1205, by which time and through the rise of Christianity, incest had become taboo. This author, rather than wanting to hide this immoral incest, probably decided to use the sin as a way to preach Christian morality; therefore, Mordred, as the result of Arthur's sin, causes Arthur's downfall.

Whether or not Mordred was conceived through incest, we must also look at who was his mother in the various versions of the legend. In Geoffrey of Monmouth, it is Arthur's sister Anna, but here Mordred is still only Arthur's nephew. In the majority of cases, after Mordred becomes the child of incest, his mother is Arthur's sister Morgause; however, since Morgause and Anna are both credited with being married to Lot of Lothian and the Orkney Isles, we can assume that Anna and Morgause are the same person.

Modern writers have sought to give Mordred still a different mother. In the Arthurian novels *Sword at Sunset* (1963) by Rosemary Sutcliff and *The Sword and the Flame: Variations on a Theme of Sir Thomas Malory* (1978) by Catherine Christian (republished in the United States as *The Pendragon*), Mordred's mother is King Arthur's half-sister Ygern. This suggestion is extremely odd since Ygern, or Igraine, is always the mother of Arthur and his sisters in the traditional versions of the legend. Arthur's mother is never even named in these two novels.

The Magdalen College Manuscript 72 of the *Chronicon de Origine et Rebus Gestis Britanniae et Angliae* says Mordred was King Arthur's son by a concubine (Fletcher 188); in Parke Godwin's novels *Firelord* (1980) and *Beloved Exile* (1984), Mordred is the son of Arthur's first wife, Morgana, who is a Pict and of no relation to Arthur (Lacy, *Arthurian Encyclopedia*, 245).

Morgan is the most popular choice after Morgause as the mother of Mordred since the two women are often conflated together as one and Arthur and Morgan traditionally have a love-hate relationship. In novels such as Philip Lindsay's *The Little Wench* (1935), Morgan is the mother of Mordred (Thompson 176). Other modern writers have made Morgan the mother of Mordred, while also trying to explain why Morgause was credited in the past with being Mordred's mother. In Marion Zimmer Bradley's *The Mists of Avalon* (1982) and in Joan Wolf's *The Road to Avalon* (1988), after Morgan gives birth to Mordred, she gives him to her sister

Morgause, who raises Mordred as her own, thus keeping with the old tradition of Morgause as Mordred's mother, while putting a new twist on the situation.

Perhaps the most interesting, although far-fetched, of the new theories surrounding the birth of Mordred lies in Norma Lorre Goodrich's study *King Arthur* (1986). Here Goodrich suggests that Mordred was actually a twin, and his twin was none other than Sir Lancelot. Goodrich points out that both Lancelot and Mordred have stories of being thrown into a body of water. Furthermore, she states that in the Celtic world, the birth of twins was considered as a sign that the mother had committed adultery with a devil. It was believed that the firstborn twin was the son of the earthly father while the second twin was the son of the Devil; giving birth to twins resulted in the mother being put to death for adultery. Beginning probably with the *Lanzelet* and carrying into later Lancelot tales, Lancelot is kidnapped by the Lady of the Lake, who then raises him as her own son. This kidnapping usually takes place when the castle of King Ban, Lancelot's father, is besieged by its enemies. Lancelot's mother flees the confusion with her child. She either sets her son down for a minute, or else she accidentally drops him into the water. The Lady of the Lake then appears and steals away the child. Goodrich suggests that this kidnapping may have been a late version of an earlier story in which Lancelot's mother, because Lancelot was the second born twin, threw her son into the lake to drown him. If she could successfully hide the fact that she had twins, she would not be put to death for sleeping with a devil (163).

However, the *Lanzelet* is the first source for this story and it is a late source. It seems unlikely that this German author would have knowledge of an actual tradition which the English, Welsh, and French writers never mentioned; therefore, it is more probable that Zatzikhoven invented this story from his own imagination than that he found it in a now lost Arthurian source.

Furthermore, the *Lanzelet* states that Lancelot is a year old when he is thrown into the lake (26). Obviously, if Lancelot were a year old, his mother would not try to drown him so late after his birth when his being a twin would already be known. Perhaps this statement of Lancelot's age, however, is also a later addition to the story. Originally, Lancelot's mother may have thrown him into the lake, and the later romancers, not understanding why a mother would so treat her child, may have added the attack upon the castle to try and make the tale understandable (Goodrich, *King Arthur*, 164-5).

Is it possible then that Lancelot was Mordred's brother and twin, and therefore, even the son of King Arthur? If so, then Lancelot's true mother was not King Ban's wife, commonly named Clarine or Helen, but Morgause or Morgan le Fay. In the *Lanzelet*, a mermaid messenger declares that Lancelot "is now proved a relative of the most generous man whom the world ever saw: King Arthur of Cardigan was beyond doubt his uncle...Thus Lanzelet discovered he was Arthur's sister's child" (92-3). If tradition says Lancelot was Arthur's nephew as Mordred is referred to as being, then is it not just as possible that he was Arthur's son born of an incestuous relationship?

This theory leaves some confusion since it doesn't seem necessary that if twins were born, the mother would have thrown both into the sea to hide her guilt. Perhaps Lancelot was the second born, believed to be the devil's son, and therefore tossed into the sea to prevent his mother's death; following this event, Arthur's edict was made, which resulted in Mordred also being tossed into the sea. Mordred was probably the first born child since in some sources his mother wished to prevent his death by casting him out in a floating cradle that allowed him to be washed ashore (Goodrich, *King Arthur*, 164). However, the cradle suggests that the writer may have merely been borrowing from other sources such as the biblical tales of Moses and the slaughter of the innocents by King Herod, or the classical tales of Perseus and Oedipus. In these tales, children are ordered to be murdered by a king because that king fears a child overthrowing him when the child becomes an adult. Similarly, Arthur is afraid of Merlin's prophecy that Mordred is the child who will result in his downfall so he orders all the children of Mordred's age to be killed. Therefore, the tale of Mordred's nearly drowning may have its origins in either biblical or classical sources, or it could be a universal motif that the Celtic people also frequently used.

   If Goodrich's theory is correct, then Lancelot was King Arthur's son, since it is doubtful he would have been the son of a devil. Something else Goodrich doesn't mention that could help back up her theory from a mythological point of view is the tale of Dylan's birth. Arianrhod is said to have given birth to two children, Dylan and another son named Llew Llaw Gyffes. Llew was a solar god who grew so rapidly that when he was four, he was as big as if he were eight, and he was the comeliest youth ever seen (Rolleston 381). If Dylan and Llew were twins, then could Mordred and Lancelot also be twins? Loomis suggests that Lancelot may have mythological connections to Llew, and his name might even be derived from Llew (*Lanzelet* 15). This connection is disputed by most present day scholars, but we will return to it in Chapter 7.

   If Lancelot is Arthur's son, there is a good possibility that he is connected to Arthur's earlier son, Llacheu, since both may have connections to solar gods. Rhys has claimed that Llacheu wore a circle of gold, and although this seems unlikely as we saw in Chapter 3, Lancelot is credited with similarly possessing a ring by the Lady of the Lake. Norma Goodrich says this ring may have been able to clear Lancelot's head since he was subject to delusions and madness (*King Arthur* 164). Although Llacheu's circle of gold does not protect or heal his head since it is chopped off, perhaps Lancelot's need for something to protect his head is a borrowed motif from Llacheu's losing his head. Goodrich also points out that Lohengrin's mother put golden chains around her babies' necks as she surrendered them to be thrown into the lake (*King Arthur* 164). This ring may then have a connection to the Lady of the Lake. If Llacheu is in some way a source for Mordred, who was also thrown into the sea, then it is not so surprising that Llacheu would have had such a ring.

   Whether or not Lancelot is Mordred's brother and Arthur's son, it is an interesting theory that has some support in Mordred's own mythological background. This background suggests that Mordred may have traditionally been Arthur's son from the beginning, a son born through incest rather than originating as a nephew who was then twisted into the child of incest by the romancers. Whether Mordred was the child of incest is not even a major issue in Arthurian studies compared to how this tale of incest may have affected Mordred's character in literature. We will now turn to statements on Mordred's character, and how it drastically changed because of the writings of Geoffrey of Monmouth and his successors.

Chapter 5: The Character of Mordred

The name of Mordred is synonymous with traitor to those familiar with the Arthurian legends. If ever a cursed figure has existed in literature, it is Mordred, for how can one feel sorry for him when he is the murderer of King Arthur, the greatest, most noble king Britain ever had? Yet Mordred was not always an evil character in the legends. In the Welsh tradition, he was even honorable and admired.

The earliest written source we have for Mordred is the tenth century *Annales Cambriae* where it states that Arthur and Mordred fell at Camlann in 539, but no mention is made of their relationship or their being on opposite sides. Mordred may only be mentioned as falling with Arthur because he was one of the highest and greatest members of King Arthur's court.

The Welsh tradition describes Mordred as one of the three kingly knights of Arthur's court, and it states that no one could deny him anything because of his courtliness. The curious qualities to which his persuasive powers were due were his calmness, mildness, and purity (Guest, *Mabinogion*, 344). Loomis also states that in a Welsh Triad Mordred is mentioned along with Nasiens, King of Denmark, as "men of such gentle, kindly, and fair words that anyone would be sorry to refuse them anything" (Loomis, *Celtic Myth*, 146-7). When the Welsh had such nice things to say about Mordred, we can hardly expect him to have become a traitor.

Whether Mordred was actually Arthur's nephew before Geoffrey of Monmouth's writings cannot be determined; in "The Dream of Rhonabwy," he is mentioned as Arthur's nephew (Jones, *Mabinogion*, 140), but this Welsh tale could have been influenced by Geoffrey of Monmouth since it was not written down until the fourteenth century. Furthermore, we must notice that Mordred is described in the above passage as a "kingly" knight, and later he is grouped with the King of Denmark. "Kingly" would seem to mean that Mordred was himself a king, or at least of royal blood. He would be royal if he were the son of Arthur's sister and King Lot; possibly, he would have even inherited a kingdom upon his father's death. In some later versions of the legend, he was supposed to inherit Arthur's throne, as will be further discussed in Chapter 9; therefore, the hint that Mordred may have been a king could be well founded.

Mordred's ability to persuade people so that none could refuse him may need to be looked at a little more hesitantly. It sounds almost as if he were capable of manipulating people, but this interpretation may be false reading between the lines in an attempt to find sarcasm where it was not intended. Such a negative interpretation was often used by the later romancers in their portraits of Mordred. They may have simply been misinterpreting what the Welsh had said of Mordred, or the person who wrote these Welsh traditions down may have been fusing the Welsh traditions with other more recent concepts of Mordred's character.

One quality attributed to Mordred that we cannot overlook is his purity. Mordred is perhaps the last character in the legends one would expect to have been pure. In Geoffrey of Monmouth, Mordred is so far from purity that he is trying to force Guinevere into marriage with him. However, the sin of marrying his father's wife is a sin Mordred originally seems innocent of having committed since it is not mentioned in any of the earlier Welsh versions of the legend.

One final clue to what may have been Mordred's true character is that the Welsh Triads give two reasons for the Battle of Camlann. One of these is the blow Gwenhyvar struck to Gwenhwyvach, said to be her sister in "Culhwch and Olwen" (Jones, *Mabinogion*, 106). The other, surprisingly enough, is the blow Arthur gave to Mordred (Guest, *Mabinogion*, 343). Here it appears as if Mordred is not even at fault, but rather Arthur! Does this statement mean Mordred is the good guy or on the right side in the battle? This interpretation may seem impossible, but we must keep it in mind because it will need to be further explored when we discuss the Battle of Camlann. Since the passage does not give Arthur's reason for striking Mordred, it could also be interpreted that Mordred started the trouble and Arthur was merely retaliating.

Although the Welsh tales do depict Mordred as rebelling against Arthur, it is strange that if they were influenced by Geoffrey of Monmouth, they would have said so many nice things about Mordred which Geoffrey does not credit to Mordred. The writing of the Welsh tales may have been influenced by Geoffrey of Monmouth's *The History of the Kings of Britain*, but they may have also been drawing on independent Welsh traditions from which Geoffrey may have also drawn. Perhaps Geoffrey only borrowed the negative aspects of Mordred's character, while *The Mabinogion* presents Mordred as a more rounded and realistic character.

Geoffrey of Monmouth's portrayal of Mordred as completely evil allowed Geoffrey's successors to exaggerate this wickedness to extremes. Mordred's character became darkest when the author of the *Mort Artu* (1205) decided to make him the child of incest. As we have seen, this incestuous birth may have been an almost forgotten tradition about Mordred; however, it also could have been invented to degrade Mordred further. A person born of incest was viewed as being nothing short of a devil by the Christian writers of the Middle Ages; these writers viewed Mordred's incestuous birth as an act of lust, and through this act of lust, even greater lust was conceived; therefore, Mordred became the most despicable, lustful character in the romances, quickly losing his last good characteristic, his purity.

A few examples of the lustful deeds attributed to Mordred during the Middle Ages can be found in the *Huth Merlin* and *Claris et Laris*. In the former, Mordred is so lacking in gratitude toward his host that he seduces the girl who is his host's *amie* (Bruce, *Evolution* vol. 2, 345). Even worse than seducing maidens, in *Claris et Laris*, Mordred attempts to rape a girl, but she is rescued before he can succeed. Later in the romance, he again attempts to rape a girl, but he is foiled in his attempt when the girl turns out to be a knight in disguise (Bruce, *Evolution* vol. 2, 271, 273). And of course Mordred

is guilty of making attempts against Guinevere, which will be
further explored in Chapters 6 and 7.

One reason why all this evil may have been attributed to
Mordred could go back to our earlier discussion of his name origins.
The Welsh form of Mordred's name was Medraut or Medrawt, but
it was later changed to Mordred, the *Mor* part of his name
suggesting connotations to various European words for the sea. The
stories of Mordred's connection to the sea may have caused writers
to believe he had some connection to death, specifically by
drowning—hence his rescue from drowning at birth, so they
borrowed from this new suggestive meaning in his name to depict
him as evil. Of course, it could be that the name change was the
result of writers wanting a name that more accurately depicted his
already established evil character. In any case, Mordred's character
makes a change for the worse at approximately the same time as his
name passes from the form of Medraut to Mordred.

Mordred's wickedness, rather than growing into a more
grotesque depiction, has received more sympathy from modern
writers. We now live in an age of psychology where we look at the
environment of the child that formed the adult. Consequently,
trying to understand Mordred's villainous behavior has provided
him with a degree of sympathy; after all, how can he help hating his
father, when that father tried to drown him, and furthermore, he
must deal with the knowledge that he is the child of incest?

In some of the modern fiction, Mordred even appears to be
regretful of his evil ways prior to the Battle of Camlann. Often he
appears to be the victim of fate, trapped in a situation he is unable
to avoid (Lacy, *Arthurian Encyclopedia*, 394). Even when he is not
a sympathetic character, some writers depict him as not being
completely at fault for the Battle of Camlann. Writers over the
centuries, from Sir Thomas Malory to Mary Stewart in her novel
The Wicked Day (1983), have arranged a meeting between Arthur
and Mordred before the Battle of Camlann. In *The Wicked Day*, it
is decided that Mordred will be king after Arthur's death and have
lands of his own until that time. In both Malory and Stewart, the
Battle of Camlann begins during this meeting. While Mordred and

Arthur are negotiating, one of their soldiers steps on an adder, which then attacks him; the soldier's reflex is to draw his sword and kill the snake. The flash of the sword, at the same time Arthur happens to raise his arm, is interpreted by the two armies as the sign to start the battle, and so the wicked day begins. Here Mordred, although desiring the kingdom, was at least trying to make peace with Arthur so there need be no more battles, but it is Mordred and Arthur's fate to slay each other, as Merlin predicted would happen when Mordred was born.

Occasionally in the modern texts, Mordred is even seen as having a purpose besides his own selfish desires for the throne. In *The Mists of Avalon* (1982), he is the arm of his mother, Morgan le Fay, sent to punish King Arthur for betraying the Isle of Avalon and forgetting his vows to the Goddess. Although Morgan seems a little fanatical at times in this work, the reader always sympathizes with her and so Mordred comes out on what is viewed as the side of good.

Perhaps the most unusual view of Mordred lies not so much in whether he was a good or an evil person, but in the theory that he, and not Arthur, was the rightful King of Britain, which would give a new understanding to his actions, making them merely an attempt to regain what was rightfully his. This interesting theory will be discussed more fully in Chapter 9. First, let us follow our chronological scheme of study and see what lies behind the tale of Mordred's abduction of Guinevere since that is generally one of the causes for the Battle of Camlann.

Chapter 6: Mordred and the Abduction of Guinevere

The only unequivocally evil deed that tradition always says Mordred was guilty of committing was trying to seize Arthur's crown. Mordred was placed in the advantageous position where he could have succeeded in this opportunity because Arthur left him as regent of the kingdom while he went to fight on the continent. In some versions, such as in Geoffrey of Monmouth, Arthur goes to battle against the Romans who wish to exact fealty from him. Later versions such as Malory's *Le Morte D'Arthur* say that after Lancelot rescued Guinevere from being burnt at the stake for committing adultery, she was proven innocent and always loyal to Arthur, so she was returned to England; however, Gawain, because Lancelot had slain his brothers, urged Arthur to fight Lancelot, so when Arthur left for France where Lancelot had sought refuge, he left Mordred in charge of the kingdom.

All versions since Geoffrey of Monmouth are clear in stating that once Arthur left, Mordred tried to seize the crown and marry Queen Guinevere to make his position stronger. The questions which must be dealt with then are why did he wish to marry Guinevere, and was the queen willing to be Mordred's wife?

Wace states that Mordred had long been in love with the queen before he was left in charge of Britain. It is not known if this situation were an early tradition that Wace was following, independent of Geoffrey, the origins of which have now been lost, or if it were merely Wace's own creation (Fletcher 141). However, it is less likely that Mordred loved Guinevere than that he thought by marrying the queen, he would gain more support as King of Britain. This strategy makes even more sense when coupled with the tradition that some, though certainly not all, Celtic tribes were matriarchal, meaning that the crown passed to the spouse of the king or chief's daughter. Norma Goodrich argues that Guinevere was not Celtic but Pictish, and it was actually the Picts, not the Celts, who followed a matriarchal tradition. Originally, it was the royal woman's right freely to bestow the chieftainship on whichever man she chose for her consort (*King Arthur* 148). John Rhys supports this idea by referring to Dio Cassius, who states:

> Pictish ladies openly consorted with the best warriors of the race....Further the Pictish succession cannot have always been confined to the Pictland of the North, for the ancient literature described abounds in heroes who are usually described with the aid of the mother's name (Goodrich, *King Arthur*, 149).

The use of the mother's name shows that a matriarchal society existed for the Picts, and therefore, royal lines were probably determined by the royal daughters' lines. By Guinevere's time, however, it was probably not uncommon for the queen simply to be kidnapped because whoever had control of her would be king. This goal was probably Mordred's purpose in attempting to marry her.

The question then is whether Guinevere was willing to marry Mordred? The romancers are split upon the issue. In the Vulgate *Mort Artu* (1205), Guinevere rejects Mordred's proposals (Lacy, *Arthurian Encyclopedia*, 394). Jehan de Warrin, in his *Recueil*, or complete history of Great Britain, begun about 1455, says that Guinevere married Mordred under compulsion (Fletcher 230). In Malory, Guinevere pretends to go along with Mordred, but before they can be married, she fortifies the Tower of London and locks herself inside it so he cannot force her into wedlock. Finally, Welsh Triad 52 states that Mordred dragged Guinevere from the throne to usurp it, and the Battle of Camlann was fought to avenge this insult; however, no mention is made here of Mordred attempting to marry Guinevere (Guest, *Mabinogion*, 319-20).

Of course, several writers believe Guinevere was not so innocent. Layamon states that when Arthur was about to return to England "the queen came to Mordred, who was to her dearest of men," to warn him of Arthur's return (261). Robert of Gloucester, in the thirteenth century, adamantly states that Guinevere was guilty rather than being a victim of Mordred's violence; he even asserts that it was at Guinevere's advice that Mordred committed treason (Fletcher 197). One minor French chronicle (Brit. MS. Addit. 11713) that follows Geoffrey of Monmouth's plot states that Guinevere was equally guilty with Mordred (Fletcher 210). In the late fourteenth century *Alliterative Morte d'Arthur*, Arthur is even slain by his own sword, Clarent, which Guinevere has had in her keeping and treacherously gives to Mordred for the Battle of Camlann (Loomis, *Celtic Myth*, 16).

All of this confusion as to whether Guinevere was loyal to Arthur while Mordred was in charge of the kingdom may be the result of Geoffrey of Monmouth's vague statements about the situation, which his various followers chose to interpret or sought to explain in different ways. Goodrich remarks that Geoffrey of Monmouth does not slander Guinevere, but merely says her second marriage to Mordred was not sanctioned by the church (*King Arthur* 101). Goodrich also states that Geoffrey said Guinevere ruled as co-regent with Mordred, but she gives no reasons for why Arthur chose them (*King Arthur* 106-7). Fletcher remarks that Geoffrey of Monmouth never openly accused Guinevere; he merely implied her guilt by not saying she resisted Mordred, and later Geoffrey states that she feared Arthur and fled from him when he returned to England (197).

Let us allow Geoffrey to speak for himself. The scene is in Allabroges as Arthur is preparing to cross the mountains and make his way to Rome.

> …when the news was brought to him that his nephew Mordred, in whose care he had left Britain, had placed the crown upon his own head. What is more, this treacherous tyrant was living adulterously and out of wedlock with Queen Guinevere, who had broken the vows of her earlier marriage.

> About this matter, most noble Duke, Geoffrey of
> Monmouth prefers to say nothing (257).

Later Mordred fights against Arthur, and then after this battle he
heads for Winchester.

> However, the Perjurer [Mordred] re-formed his army
> and so marched into Winchester on the following night.
> When this was announced to Queen Guinevere, she gave
> way to despair. She fled from York to the City of the
> Legions and there, in the church of Julius the Martyr, she
> took her vows among the nuns, promising to lead a chaste
> life (259).

Then Arthur "marched on the third day to the city of Winchester
and laid siege to his nephew who had taken refuge there" (259).

In the first passage, Mordred is living in adultery with Guinevere,
and she is implied as being equally guilty because it clearly states she
has broken the vows of her first marriage. Geoffrey's refusal to
make any more comment on it sounds as if the deeds of these two
people were so wicked he could not write in more detail about
them.

Fletcher says that Guinevere flees from Arthur, but actually
Guinevere is in York at this time, and she flees to a nunnery in
Caerleon, a place much closer to Winchester than is York. She is
probably not so much fleeing from Arthur, as she is fleeing to a
nunnery where she will receive clemency if Arthur defeats Mordred
and then attempts to punish her. However, in the second passage it
is not Arthur but Mordred who enters Winchester, and it is upon
hearing that Mordred is in the city that she flees to a convent. It is
doubtful that Guinevere is fleeing from Mordred since her
movements are only bringing her closer to him. Instead, her fleeing
to a nunnery seems to imply her guilt; it is also possible that if
Arthur, not knowing she had been in York, finds her in a nunnery in
Caerleon, he might feel that her presence there implies her innocence. Therefore, Guinevere could be trying to play innocent when
she is actually guilty of being Mordred's accomplice. Of course, she
could have also been confident that Arthur would defeat Mordred,

so rather than being miles from him, Guinevere decided to go to a nunnery where Arthur could more easily reach her after he won the battle.

If Guinevere had had a spotless reputation prior to this event, we would probably be willing to believe in her innocence, but let us first examine the various indiscretions with which other writers have credited her.

If a tradition existed of Guinevere's being adulterous with anyone other than Mordred before the time of Geoffrey of Monmouth, that tradition has not come down to us, and as already stated, it remains questionable whether she is intended to be adulterous in Geoffrey of Monmouth. In fact, Marie, Countess of Champagne, seems to be the one responsible for creating the liasion between Guinevere and Lancelot (Lacy, *Arthurian Encyclopedia*, 263). Since then, Lancelot has remained the most prominent of Guinevere's lovers, but some writers have credited her with having others. In the *Mort Artu*, Lancelot takes Mordred's place as Guinevere's lover (Bruce, *Evolution*, vol. 1, 439). Another tradition says that Gawaine was Guinevere's lover (*Lanzelet* 206), and Kay, as we saw in Chapter 3, might also be considered a likely candidate.

Other examples of Guinevere's adultery, although perhaps less well-known, are still abundant in the romances. In Chrétien de Troyes' *Erec*, Morgain has a lover named Guiamor de Camelide. Guinevere discovers the lovers and warns them that if Arthur finds out, Guiamor will be in danger. Guiamor then deserts Morgain and becomes Guinevere's lover, perhaps just to keep her quiet. The result, of course, is that Morgain hates Guinevere, especially since Morgain later bears Guiamor a son (Paton 61).

Another example is in Marie de France's *Lay of Lanval* where Guinevere does not actually commit adultery, but she would have if she had had her way. She makes an offer of love to Lanval, but he refuses her because he already has a mistress and he will not do wrong to his king by accepting her. In anger, Guinevere then accuses him of insulting her, and he is arrested (Cross 586; Bruce, *Evolution*, vol. 2, 170). This story is actually a version of the biblical story of Joseph and Potiphar's wife, which was so well known it was frequently reused throughout the Middle Ages both in Arthurian and other literary works (Bruce, *Evolution*, vol. 2., 170). Another example of this motif is the tale of *Graelent*, where again the knight refuses the queen. The only difference there being that when the queen speaks ill of him to the king, the king refuses to pay him for fighting in the wars (Cross 587).

Guinevere is not always so forward. In *Claris et Laris*, written about 1268, the knight Claris is visited by Guinevere when he is wounded; he makes love to her, although she does rebuke him (Bruce, *Evolution*, vol. 2, 267). In the French romance *Yder* (circa the 1220s), Arthur is jealous of the knight Yder, and when he asks Guinevere whom she would remarry if he died, she replies that she would remarry Yder (Bruce, *Evolution*, vol. 2, 222).

In some works, Arthur does not even get angry about Guinevere's lovers, particularly not Lancelot. In the *Huth Merlin* (thirteenth century), Arthur says that he would rather have Lancelot and Guinevere married than lose Lancelot's companionship (Bruce, *Evolution*, vol. 2, 338). Here Guinevere's fidelity is not as important to Arthur as his friendship for Lancelot. A similar theme has been adopted by modern chroniclers of the legend; for example in the film *Camelot* (1967), Arthur knows Guinevere and Lancelot have betrayed him, yet he loves them both and wishes to keep everything calm, so he continually ignores their relationship until he can ignore it no longer. In *The Mists of Avalon* (1982), Arthur believes his and Guinevere's failure to bear a child may be his own inability to father a child since he does not yet know he has a son, Mordred. In order to have an heir, Arthur actually leads Lancelot and Guinevere to bed together and lies with them. Later in the novel, Guinevere remarks to Arthur that she saw how he touched Lancelot, which leads us to suspect that Arthur loves Lancelot so much he can no less bear to be parted from his friend than from his queen, so he allows the two lovers to commit adultery. Bradley is bringing to the surface an often noticed idea that Arthur was possibly bisexual because of his friendship with Lancelot. Perhaps Arthur sleeps with Guinevere and Lancelot not because he wants an heir, but simply because he desires to be with Lancelot. In such a case, Guinevere would not be the adulterer, but merely the tool Arthur uses so he can lie with the man he desires.

Another lover whom modern writers have attributed to Guinevere is Bedwyr, or Bedivere. He was Arthur's right-hand in the earlier legends, but later his position was usurped by the popularity of Lancelot. No early tradition exists of Bedivere committing adultery with Guinevere. However, Lancelot replaced Bedivere in the legends, and then became Guinevere's lover. In *Sword at Sunset* (1963), Rosemary Sutcliff decided to replace Lancelot with the original greatest knight Bedivere. However, Sutcliff also decided that Bedivere, or Bedwyr, would be Guinevere's lover even though he had no relationship with Guinevere in the earlier versions. Gillian Bradshaw, Mary Stewart, and Joan Wolf have all followed this pattern, so Lancelot must now compete with Bedwyr in the modern fiction for a place in the queen's embrace (Lacy, *Arthurian Encyclopedia*, 43).

Some authors and scholars argue that Guinevere really was a faithful and chaste wife. Lacy points out that the *Lanzelet* contains no suggestion of adulterous love between Lancelot and Guinevere (*Arthurian Handbook* 110). Norma Goodrich, Guinevere's staunchest supporter, boldly states that nothing in the old romances indicates that Lancelot received any tokens of love from Guinevere, and she tries to support this argument by quoting from Malory (*Guinevere* 125).

> But nowadays men cannot love seven nights but they must have all their desires: that love may not endure by reason; for where they be soon accorded and hasty, heat soon it cooleth. Right so fareth love nowadays, soon hot, soon cold: this is no stability. But the old love was not so; men and women could love together seven years, and no licours lusts were between them, and then was love, truth, and faithfulness: and lo, in likewise was used love in King Arthur's days (Malory, vol. 2, 426).

Goodrich also points out that in Chrétien de Troyes' writings, all Lancelot possessed of Guinevere's was the hair he had taken from her comb (*Guinevere* 125). However, Goodrich is willfully ignoring some of the key passages in Chrétien such as in *Lancelot, or the Knight of the Cart* where Lancelot enters Guinevere's bed. I quote from Kibler's translation.

> Now Lancelot had his every wish;
> The queen willingly
> Sought his company and comfort,
> As he held her in his arms,
> And she held him in hers.
> Her love-play seemed so gentle and good to him,
> Both her kisses and caresses,
> That in truth the two of them felt
> A joy and wonder,
> The equal of which had never
> Yet been heard or known.
> But I shall ever keep it secret,
> Since it should not be written of:
> The most delightful
> And choicest pleasure is that
> Which is hinted, but never told.
> Lancelot had great joy
> And pleasure all that night (l. 4669-86)

As Chrétien says "The most delightful/And choicest pleasure is that/Which is hinted." Obviously, Lancelot and Guinevere were not as innocent in the old romances as Goodrich would like to pretend.

Norma Goodrich even argues that Guinevere and Arthur's marriage was never consummated, but this assertion would be completely ignoring the possibility that Guinevere was Llacheu's mother. Goodrich makes this argument to support her bizarre theory that Guinevere was actually a high-priestess of the grail and therefore virginal (*Guinevere* 171). Goodrich's theory seems extremely doubtful since the king would want his wife to provide him with an heir, so why would he have married a high priestess? Even if Arthur had kidnapped Guinevere, it is doubtful the marriage would not have been consummated since he probably would have forced her into it if she were his queen because it was her duty to provide him with an heir. Even if she refused him, by medieval law and custom, the man had the right to force his wife into having sexual relations with him.

Norma Goodrich's other theory is that Guinevere's reputation has been ruined due to mistranslations. She says that certain Gaelic words were linguistically prone to mistranslation. She cites the Irish scholar John Toland, who points out that when ancient Irish writers spoke of a bed, they very often meant an altar, so everytime Lancelot is said to be going to Guinevere's bed, he was actually going to her altar. She was the priestess for whom he was the acolyte (Goodrich, *Guinevere*, 172). This error seems much too large to have been made even if bed and altar were similar words. More likely the romancers were following the courtly love motif in which the religious and secular lives were combined so that a bed of love would be approached with the same reverence as an altar, since in both places a form of sacrament is consummated. Lancelot and Guinevere traditionally do enter holy orders at the end of their lives which may reflect not simply penance for their sins, but also that they were two devoutly religious people. Lancelot, especially, is depicted as a holy person since even though he does not achieve the Holy Grail, he is one of the very few knights who acquires a second sight of it. However, since Goodrich suggested in *King Arthur* that Guinevere was a Pictish queen who could choose her own lovers, her arguments that Guinevere was also a virginal high priestess of the Holy Grail are not convincing.

Two other possible arguments have been made against Guinevere being an adulteress. Norma Goodrich suggests that Bedivere may have been Guinevere's brother, although again she does not state why she thinks so (*Guinevere* 39). However, it is not until the modern fiction that Guinevere and Bedivere are coupled together, so without an early source, it is unlikely that Guinevere ever committed adultery with Bedivere. Another strange tradition says that Guinevere and Mordred were brother and sister (Fletcher 141). This relationship cannot be reconciled with those of the other characters, but if we consider Mordred in his most evil persona, it is doubtful he would allow the fact that Guinevere was his sister to prevent him from marrying her and gaining a throne. It is also possible that when Wace states Mordred loved the queen before he was left in charge of Britain, he means that Mordred loved her as if he were her brother (Fletcher 141); Mordred as Guinevere's actual brother remains an extremely unlikely possibility, and if Mordred loved her as if he were her brother, he would not have attempted forcing her into marriage.

As already stated, if Guinevere were a Celtic queen, she would possibly follow the tradition of the Celtic queens to choose their own consorts, and it does not seem that queens were limited to monogamy once the first choice was made. Other Celtic queens have had many lovers, such as Queen Maeve of Connacht (Cross 635); however, both the Christian and Roman influences in sixth century Britian would have promoted monogamous relationships, so it is doubtful Guinevere would have openly taken lovers outside of her marriage. Celtic queens could also be warriors. If Guinevere were one, then it would not be surprising for her to join Mordred in planning the attack against Arthur. Lady Charlotte Guest remarks that in Geoffrey of Monmouth, before the Battle of Camlann, Arthur had his army divided into nine divisions; Guest suggests that Guinevere may have possibly been a commander over one of these divisions (*Mabinogion* 322). Even more striking is the statement in the *Prose Lancelot* that Guinevere collected the heads of her enemies, which was a common Celtic practice (*King Arthur* 115). Guinevere would seem to have been an able warrior rather than a stay-at-home queen, and therefore, certainly capable of playing a major role in plotting with Mordred against King Arthur. However, Goodrich does not tell us from where Guinevere collected her heads, so it is far more likely the heads were gifts to her from her subjects or admirers than that she actually went into battle to behead her enemies.

Any queen who had as many affairs as are credited to Guinevere would most likely have become pregnant. Guinevere would not have had to worry about having illegitimate children if she were barren as many of the legends state. However, it still seems most reasonable that in Welsh tradition Guinevere was the mother of Llacheu. If Guinevere could bear one child, she probably could have had more. Wace is the first writer to state that Arthur and Guinevere could not have an heir. He may have simply been clarifying why Geoffrey of Monmouth never mentions that the couple had any children. It is possible that Wace did not know the Welsh tradition that Arthur had had sons, but it is also likely he chose to ignore it as Geoffrey did (Fletcher 140-1).

The romancers probably found it convenient for Arthur and Guinevere to have no children, and they explained this lack of children as Guinevere being barren. If a child were born to the couple, the writer would have had to find a way for the child to die before the Battle of Camlann, so Mordred could be made regent while Arthur was away on the continent. Guinevere's barrenness made it especially convenient for all the affairs that were invented for her. It would have been awkward for Guinevere to have had several illegitimate children without Arthur suspecting anything. It is possible that Arthur might have overlooked one illegitimate child to ensure that he had an heir, but in the Middle Ages, it would have been unthinkable for the heir to the throne not to be the monarch's closest male relative. Furthermore, Arthur has plenty of nephews to succeed him, so Arthur's not having a son may not have been as large a problem as is often depicted. It is not until the modern fiction that any author even suggests Guinevere could have had children that were not Arthur's.

In Richard Hovey's *The Birth of Galahad* (1898), Guinevere is the mother of Lancelot's son, Galahad, but the play actually shifts away from the birth so that it never becomes a real conflict. In Susan Cooper's *The Grey King* (1976), we learn that Guinevere had betrayed her lord once before, and he found out, but it is only vaguely hinted that Arthur knew of Guinevere's adultery because she had an illegitimate child. We only get this information because Guinevere wishes to hide her newborn child, which is Arthur's, for fear that he will think it is another man's and have it put to death. Further discussion of this novel will be in Chapter 16 on modern Arthurian fiction.

However, just because Guinevere may have been in the habit of committing adultery does not necessarily mean she would have agreed to commit adultery with Mordred. Perhaps the best argument that Guinevere was not Mordred's accomplice lies in the earliest traditions, before the romances blotted her name with all the accusations of adultery against her.

According to the *Perlesvaus*, Guinevere dies from grief over the death of her son Loholt, and her death occurs while Arthur's glory is still at its height (Bruce, *Evolution*, vol. 2, 19). In the *Lancelot* ms., Guinevere also dies before Arthur's wars with Mordred (Bruce, *Evolution*, vol. 2, 150).

Norma Goodrich remarks in *King Arthur* that the story of the exhumation of Arthur and Guinevere at Glastonbury releases Guinevere from a slanderous marriage to Mordred; furthermore, Guinevere was already dead and buried at the time of Arthur's continental campaign (133). If Guinevere had betrayed Arthur, it is doubtful he would have allowed her to be buried with him, but since the finding of their bodies at Glastonbury was most likely a publicity stunt, and not the true grave of either Arthur or Guinevere, we cannot be sure whether they were buried together. Norma Goodrich continues to discuss the queen's death in *Guinevere*, where she says the English accounts that Guinevere died in a nunnery inside England are false, particularly because Southern England was being overrun by pagan Saxons at the time (201). Therefore, Guinevere may have already died before Arthur since the Saxons were being held at bay during Arthur's reign.

The solution of what, if any, part Guinevere played in the events that led to Arthur's fall may never be solved. Scholars will have to weigh the evidence for both sides and decide for themselves, but I personally feel the most antiquated version, the Welsh stories, is probably the closest to the truth. Therefore, if a historical Guinevere ever lived, she probably was the mother to Arthur's children, did not commit adultery, and died before Camlann, meaning she was innocent of all the charges brought against her.

Chapter 7: Arthur, Mordred, and Guinevere: A Romantic Triangle

Arthur and Mordred first appear in the tenth century *Annales Cambriae*, in which they are simply said to have fallen at Camlann in 539. The creators of legend, or those whom tradition has supplied with more detail than what this simple statement tells us, wrote that Arthur and Mordred were either father and son or uncle and nephew who fought against each other for a kingdom and a queen.

The fight between two men for a woman has never been uncommon, but to make the relationship between these two men be father and son is adding a twist to an old tale. Not a new twist, however, for we have already seen how often mythological stories and characters were transposed onto Arthurian characters, and in the case of the Battle of Camlann and what led up to it, this borrowing from earlier myths probably happened more thoroughly than any other time in the legends.

The father and son combat, or the combat over a woman, is an ancient story found throughout world myths, but especially in Celtic mythology, the foundation for so much of the Arthurian material.

Among the many Celtic tales that are similar to the Mordred, Arthur, and Guinevere triangle is the tale of Midir and Etain (see the discussion in Chapter 4). Midir as the origin of Mordred seems even more probable when we look at the tales concerning him.

Midir tries to abduct Etain from her husband Eochaid because Etain was Midir's wife when she was in an earlier incarnation. Eochaid, not realizing that Midir wants to steal Etain, agrees when Midir suggests they play fidchell, a form of chess. They play several games, Midir always allowing Eochaid to win until Eochaid believes himself the better player. Then Midir proposes one final game, the stakes to be whatever the victor names when the game is over. Midir wins, and then he declares his prize will be that he may hold Etain in his arms and receive a kiss from her. Eochaid tells him to return one month from the day to receive his wish.

Eochaid, however, fears evil and surrounds the palace with a band of armed men on the appointed day so Midir cannot enter. Despite the safeguards, Midir mysteriously appears in the palace, places his arm around Etain, turns them both into swans, and they fly away from the castle.

Eochaid, who wants Etain back, discovers she is with Midir in a fairy mound he then attacks. Midir now offers to give up Etain, but he sends her back with fifty handmaidens who all look like her. Etain, however, has given Eochaid a sign to know her by, so that he regains his queen and the couple live together until her death, ten years later. Etain bears one daughter to Eochaid who is also named Etain (Rolleston 156-63).

This tale may very well be the oldest source, or the original source for the story of Mordred and Arthur fighting for Guinevere. Of course, it also seems close to the tales of Arthur fighting Lancelot. When Eochaid tries to defend his castle against Midir's attack, one is reminded of how Arthur planned to burn Guinevere at the stake, but then Lancelot breaks through Arthur's guard to rescue her. When Eochaid then chases after the couple to Midir's fairy mound, we are reminded of Arthur laying siege to Lancelot's castle of La Joyeuse Gard where Lancelot and Guinevere have retreated. One significant aspect of Midir's tale is the game of chess played to win the maiden, which we will see repeated later when Guinevere plays chess with Melwas in an effort to protect herself.

The Celtic tale of the Irish God of Light, Lugh, also parallels not only the conflict between Arthur and Mordred, but most of Mordred's story. We have already discussed the tale of Dylan and how it corresponds with that of Mordred's birth, and that Dylan's brother Llew was a sun god. The Irish god Lugh was simply another version of the god Llew with a somewhat similar tale. In Lugh's tale, the Fomorian King Balor hears in a Druidic prophecy that he will be slain by his own grandson. To stop the prophecy from becoming true, Balor locks his sole daughter Ethlinn in a tower and only allows her to have female companions. Then Balor steals a cow belonging to Kian. In order to get revenge on Balor, Kian seeks the advice of a druidess named Birag. Birag advises him to dress in woman's garb and go to the tower where Ethlinn is, begging for shelter. Kian gains access to Ethlinn, and of course, he gets her pregnant, the result being that Ethlinn bears him three sons.

Balor, angered at what has happened, orders the children to be drowned. The messenger, charged with this command, rolls the three children into a sheet and carries them to the appointed place to be drowned in a whirlpool. However, one child drops out and falls into a little bay. The other two children, one of whom would be the equivalent of the god Dylan, are drowned. The child in the bay, however, is rescued by the druidess, and given to Kian to raise.

Up to this point, the tale corresponds with that of Mordred. Mordred, however, is usually connected to Dylan, the analogue of whom in this tale drowns. But in Dylan's own tale, as we already saw in Chapter 4, Dylan did not actually drown, but jumped into the water. Since Dylan became a sea god, his drowning in this tale should really be interpreted as his becoming a being capable of living underwater. Lugh does not drown because he is not a sea god, as Mordred's origins seem to suggest. Instead, Lugh is a solar god, so it would make no sense for him to drown. He is rescued from the water by a druidess who has magical powers. Could she be an early version of the Arthurian Lady of the Lake and Lugh be an early form of Lancelot? If Lugh and Dylan can be interpreted as brothers, then could not Lancelot and Mordred also be brothers? Norma Goodrich's theory seems somewhat far-fetched, but here is an analogue to it in Celtic myth!

The tale continues until eventually Balor and Lugh meet and Lugh hurls into Balor's eye a great stone that kills him (Rolleston 110-17). Of course, it is not necessary to point out the similarities between Lugh and the Greek hero Perseus, who kills his grandfather by hurling a discus at the Olympics. The stone that Lugh throws also reminds one of David and Goliath. Several similar examples of such conflicts in mythology make this story a universal motif rather than a case of one tale influencing another; however, Balor and Lugh's tale may contain the greatest similarities between Arthur and Mordred's, so if the Arthurian father-son combat has a source, Balor and Lugh's tale seems the most likely candidate.

Midir's tale was one of a battle over a woman, and Lugh's tale is of a boy slaying his grandfather, but as the stories of these two separate characters continue, we find a relationship that could be combined into a more complete tale.

Lugh was said to have been the father of the greatest hero in Celtic mythology, Cuchulain (Rolleston 123). Cuchulain has a tale that closely corresponds to the Persian tale of Sohrab and Rustem. In both tales, the father slays his son, whom he does not recognize when they battle. As Rustem slays his son Sohrab, so Cuchulain slays his son Connla. Recognition in both stories is not achieved because when identities are asked, the characters refuse to reveal their names. Cuchulain, however, lives after he slays his son, unlike King Arthur.

Cuchulain has another similar tale to the fight for a maiden in which he kidnaps the flower maiden Blathnat and slays her husband Curoi. Here is where we get the connection between Lugh and Midir's tales because in at least one version, Blathnat is said to have been the daughter of Midir (Loomis, *Celtic Myth*, 327). The generational slayings continue when Curoi's son, Lewy, seeks vengeance and murders Cuchulain, cutting off his head. The beheading of a character frequently appears in Arthurian and other legends.

Loomis, in *Celtic Myth and Arthurian Romance*, points out an almost exact parallel in Welsh tradition to the conflict between Curoi and Cuchulain over Blathnat. In this version, the god Gwynn and Gwylhyr must fight every May 1st until Judgment Day for the maiden Kreiddylat (80). The date of May 1st immediately suggests a connection to Mordred, since it is traditionally his birthday. In *Wales and the Arthurian Legend*, Loomis states that the Battle on May 1st is actually between summer and winter, between the old year and the new, representing life rising out of death. This idea can be found in *The Mabinogion* when Arawn, King of Annwn, his name meaning winter and the name of his land being that of the underworld, is oppressed by Hafgan, who is summer white. Pwyll meets Arawn and takes his place in battle one year later, giving summer white one fatal blow (81). During the time Pwyll takes Arawn's place, he also respects Arawn's wife, never going to bed with her. Mordred's birth on May Day is symbolic because in the Celtic world the night before May 1st was the Eve of Beltane, the festival of the Celtic God of Death. May 1st is also a day that traditionally represents new birth. Mordred's birth symbolizes new life, but it is also connected to Beltane because with Mordred's birth will come death. Metaphorically speaking, Mordred's birth is Arthur's death because Mordred will be the cause of Arthur's death.

The tale of Pwyll and Arawn later became a source for the tale of *Sir Gawain and the Green Knight*, in which Gawain is challenged to fight the Green Knight at the end of a year. Before the year ends, he becomes guest at a castle and is placed in a position where he could lie with his host's wife, yet he abstains. The fight in *Sir Gawain and the Green Knight*, rather than taking place on May 1st, has been changed to January 1st, which is even more obvious to modern readers as the day when the old year turns into the new. Furthermore, Loomis points out that Gawain's origins seem to go back to Curoi (Loomis, *Wales*, 78). Another connection between Gawain and the Battle of Camlann is that Mordred slays his brother Gawain in the *Alliterative Morte Arthure* (l.3656-8). Although Mordred is not the actual person who murders Gawain in other versions of the legend, Mordred is still guilty of his brother's death because if Mordred had not rebelled against Arthur, no battle would have been fought where Gawain was slain. Another story of one brother slaying another is the Norse myth where Balder (like Gawain, a solar deity or representative of light) is slain by his brother Hoder (Rhys 14).

Other possible mythological sources behind the Battle of Camlann can be found in the Irish story of Elotha and Bres, and in the Breton lais of *Doon* and *Milun*, where combats are fought between father and son, ending in mutual recognition (Loomis, *Celtic Myth*, 76). In the tale of Noine, Noine's birth coincides with the death of his grandfather, Dare. Eochaid Bres (mentioned earlier in Chapter 4) was the offspring of the son and daughter of Delbaeth, and the unwitting opponent of his father in swordplay (Loomis, *Celtic Myth*, 341). The tale of Diarmuid and Grainne has also already been discussed. Finally, along with the Greek story of Perseus is the tale of the Greek God Cronus who was so afraid his children would kill him that he proceeded to eat them as they were born; however, before Zeus could be devoured, he slew his father and then set his brothers and sisters free from their father's insides.

Certainly, enough stories exist in Celtic mythology, not to mention world mythology, to serve as sources or at least as analogues for Mordred and Arthur's combat and Guinevere's involvement in it, but why the popularity of these father-son combats, and what is the meaning behind them?

The father-son combat has been interpreted by Frazer as the savage custom of an annual belief in sacrificing the king who represents the god of vegetation. Macalister has shown that a similar tradition existed among the early Irish. Other scholars, looking at all the Irish kings, omitting the Fir Bolg and Tuatha De Danaan kings, have pointed out that of one hundred and ten kings, eighty were killed by their successors. Confused historians have interpreted this information as connotating a type of generational blood feud, not realizing a tradition of sacrifices existed. A blood feud was the easiest way to explain these combats, so the genealogies were manipulated to make those who joined in combat appear to be related (Loomis, *Celtic Myth*, 79). Traditionally, each king appears to have been killed by his successor, somewhat in a similar way to the leader of an animal herd being defeated by the next leader.

Of course, the conflict between father and son does not need to have such a complicated reason behind it. Most people will agree that friction frequently exists between fathers and sons. Freud may have been the first person to explore the psychological reasons for this type of conflict, but it certainly existed long before Freud's time.

Because this father-son conflict is constantly experienced in many families, it proves that a literary or mythological source for it is really not necessary; it could easily be historical fact, or the invention of a person who had his own conflict with either his father or son.

By the time father-son combats appeared in the Arthurian legend, they did not always result in one or both of the combatants being killed. Except for the Mordred/Arthur combat, combats that were fought between fathers and sons were due to their failure to recognize each other, and they would happily end with a mutual recognition. Such combats occurred between Guiglan and his father Gawain, between Lancelot and Galahad, and between Degare and his father. Loomis points out that Gawain and Guiglan may have origins in Curoi and Cuchulain respectively, as reflected in the similarities between Guiglan and Cuchulain's names (*Celtic Myth* 77); however, all scholars no longer agree with this derivation, so despite the similarity, it is doubtful that Curoi and Cuchulain are the primary source for Gawain and Guiglan. By the Welsh stage of these tales, it even became common to have father and son, or junior-senior combats where the opponents shared the same name, as with Galahad and Lancelot, who was also named Galahad (Loomis, *Celtic Myth*, 77).

Father and son combats were common during the Middle Ages, as happened when William the Conqueror came near to killing his own son, Robert of Normandy, because their armor prevented them from recognizing each other (Bruce, *Evolution vol. 1*, 413). In the actual Arthurian era of roughly 500 A.D., armor was not so elaborate that soldiers could not always be recognized, but by the high and late Middle Ages, when the Arthurian legends became popular, armor was so elaborate that writers could easily use it as a way of preventing recognition between friends or relatives who were to do combat.

Still, the conflict between Mordred and Arthur is not the first such conflict to arise in the Arthurian legends. It may have been born out of two earlier conflicts in its own cycle, which probably originated in Celtic myth. These sources may have been the Tristan stories, and Guinevere's abduction by Melwas.

Geoffrey of Monmouth is the one responsible for making Mordred the abductor of Guinevere, but Geoffrey does not include the Tristan tale in his work. Even though Tristan was a later addition to the Arthurian cycle, the story was probably known by Geoffrey so he could have easily borrowed from it. If we follow the tradition that Mordred is Arthur's nephew, it is easy to see the parallels between Arthur and Mordred and the conflict between Tristan and King Mark. Tristan, nephew to King Mark of Cornwall, is sent by his uncle to fetch Mark's bride, Isolde. We do not have a tale of Mordred bringing Guinevere to Arthur, but Lancelot serves as an emissary, and this first meeting is generally when Lancelot and Guinevere fall in love, as Tristan and Isolde fall in love when drinking the love potion. Later, Tristan ends up marrying another Isolde, doubtless because she has the same name as the woman he loves; however, he cannot forget the first Isolde, who is now married to his uncle. This story reminds us of Lancelot sleeping with Elaine, yet never able to forget Guinevere. Rhys even suggests that the more than one Isolde, and even the tradition of the three Guineveres, may have its source in the multiple Etains (37); however, this theory seems unlikely since if there were multiple Guineveres, they were three separate people, and not various incarnations of the same person as is the case with Etain. Tristan then returns to take up his love affair with the first Isolde. King Mark finds out about the adulterous romance and murders Tristan, as Mordred murders Arthur.

The second possible source for Arthur and Mordred's conflict over Guinevere is the tale of Guinevere's abduction by Melwas or Meleagraunce. Melwas makes his first appearance in Caradoc's "life" of Gildas, written about 1130. Here Melwas is king of the Summer Land (Somereset), and he carries off Guinevere, keeping her in his stronghold at Glastonbury while Gildas lived in the neighborhood (Lacy, *Arthurian Handbook*, 375). Caradoc was almost contemporary with Geoffrey of Monmouth so Geoffrey would have had easy access to Caradoc's work. We have already discussed the possibility, from the Welsh dialogue of the fourteenth century between Arthur and Guinevere, that Kay may have been the original abductor of Guinevere. However, in most versions, he is with the queen's party when they are captured, and Kay is wounded. Later when Lancelot pricks his finger while coming to rescue Guinevere and then leaves blood stains, it is believed that since Kay is the wounded one, he entered Guinevere's bed, although in most tales, he is too wounded for it to have been possible. Since he was with the queen originally, it is possible he was the original abductor and wounded by Guinevere's rescuer. However, it is far more likely that Melwas was Guinevere's original abductor as he has remained to the present day. Generally, the one who rescues Guinevere is Lancelot, although it originally may have been King Arthur as the Welsh dialogue points out (Bruce, *Evolution* vol. 1, 196, 205).

Another tradition that has arisen with Guinevere's abduction is the game of chess she plays with her abductor, Melwas. This scene may very well be a direct borrowing from the chess game played between Midir and Eochaid for the possession of Etain, only here Guinevere plays for the right to possess her own body.

In both this tale and those we have seen of Gawain and the Green Knight, and Pwyll taking Arawn's place, the woman always keeps her chastity (Loomis, *Wales*, 85). Still, some modern versions, such as Marion Zimmer Bradley's *The Mists of Avalon* (1982), allow Melwas to rape Guinevere, and this brutal rape then becomes the reason why Guinevere is barren. One other interesting point in *The Mists of Avalon* is that Melwas claims to be Guinevere's half-brother, a bastard of her father. We have earlier discussed Wace's statement that Mordred loved the queen before he was left as regent of Britain, and Fletcher says this statement may have been an interpolation of an earlier tradition that Mordred was Guinevere's brother (Fletcher 141).

If there were a traditional blood relationship between Guinevere and Melwas, it may be that when Mordred replaced Melwas as Guinevere's abductor, which first happens in Geoffrey of Monmouth (Fletcher 94), this relationship also confusedly remained in Wace's mind.

As Mordred supplanted Melwas, so Arthur seems to have been replaced by Lancelot as Guinevere's rescuer. Some writers, taking all these different stories and trying to combine them into one specific story, have combined Lancelot and Arthur's roles. In *The Road to Avalon* (1988), Joan Wolf, following Rosemary Sutcliff and Mary Stewart's examples, replaces Lancelot with his earlier version, Bedwyr. It is Bedwyr who rescues Guinevere, but rather than slaying Meleagraunt, Bedivere merely holds him prisoner until Arthur arrives. Arthur then fights and kills Meleagraunt in a duel. Since Bedwyr does the rescuing, and Arthur does the killing, Arthur is at least being partially restored to his position as Guinevere's champion.

Another person who has become embroiled in this abduction of Guinevere is Maelgwn Gwynedd, King of North Wales. In some tales, Urien, King of Rheged tries to force Guinevere into marrying him, before she has the marriage offer of Arthur. In the film *Guinevere* (1994), Maelgwyn instead wages war on Guinevere's kingdom, trying to force her into marriage after she has already refused him. Arthur, again rather than Lancelot, arrives with his army and defeats Maelgwn, and Guinevere then agrees to marry Arthur.

The use of Maelgwn as an abductor can be traced back to the descriptions which Gildas gives of him in the sixth century. Maelgwn is said to have fought against his own uncle and knights who were young lions. He also put away his wife and murdered his nephew. He had for his instructor "the most eloquent master of almost all Britain" yet these teachings did not turn him from evil (321). Professor Sayce has argued that the uncle whom Maelgwn is accused of having slain and superseded was none other than King Arthur. If he did slay Arthur, it would explain why Gildas calls Maelgwn "insularis droco" the dragon or war captain of the island, and also why Maelgwn's successors were called by the Welsh not merely *gwledigs*, but kings although their greatest ancestor Cuneda was only a *gwledig*. However, since Gildas does not even give the uncle's name, it may be that he was no more illustrious than his predecessors, of which King Arthur was probably one (Rhys 8).

Whatever the case, the Arthurian legend had an early abduction tale, probably originating with Guinevere being abducted by Melwas and rescued by Arthur. Later this tale developed into an opportunity to begin Lancelot and Guinevere's love affair so that Arthur would fight against Lancelot; also included were Mordred's attempts against the queen, which led to the Battle of Camlann. Whatever the traditions or myths behind it, almost every version of the Arthurian legends ends with the disaster at the Battle of Camlann; therefore, what happened at Camlann and its after effects are left to be explored to complete our analysis of Arthur's most famous son.

Chapter 8: The Battle of Camlann

What happened at Camlann and after? Generally, Arthur and Mordred kill each other, Bedivere throws Arthur's sword, Excalibur, into the lake, and Arthur is carried away to Avalon. Then Guinevere, Lancelot, and some other knights enter holy orders, Constantine becomes king of Britain, and we are left with the promise that Arthur is the once and future king, the king who will come again at the hour of Britain's greatest need. This version is the most popular, but it is not the only one, and it may not even be closest to the truth.

The first question we need to ask is where was the Battle of Camlann? Most sources state that it was somewhere in Cornwall. Some scholars have supported this statement by saying that the name Mordred or Modred, which replaced the original Welsh forms of the name, Medraut or Medrawt, is Cornish and implies a Cornish tradition that the battle may have been fought in that vicinity (Lacy, *Arthurian Encyclopedia*, 78). However, we have already seen that some scholars believe the name change reflects the Anglo-Saxon influence of such names as Aelfred and Aethelred (Rhys 392).

O.G.S. Crawford and P.K. Johnstone argue that the battle was fought on Hadrian's Wall (Goodrich, *Merlin*, 91). This theory makes sense if we follow the Scottish traditions behind Mordred which we will explore in the next chapter. Crawford and Johnstone also make a very strange statement that during the battle Arthur was killed not by his son or nephew, Mordred, but rather by Vortigern's granddaughter's husband Mordred (Goodrich, *Merlin*, 91). Although this idea is unlikely, we will also return to it in Chapter 10.

In the *Didot Percival* is the curious statement that Arthur's last battle, fought against Mordred, took place in Ireland (Loomis, *Celtic Myth*, 16). This mistake may be understandable considering the influence of all the Irish myths we explored in the last chapter as possible sources for the conflict between Arthur and Mordred.

One final place that might be considered is Ercing, Hereford where Arthur is said to have slain and buried his son, Amr. This story is possibly the oldest version of the father-son combat in the Arthurian legends, and this single combat may have been exaggerated into the Battle of Camlann. The tenth century *Annales Cambriae* mentions Camlann and gives Mordred's rather than Amr's name, but because no evidence exists here that Arthur and Mordred are related or are on opposite sides, the *Annales Cambriae* could have been independent of influence from Nennius. Geoffrey of Monmouth could have borrowed Amr's story from Nennius and then replaced Amr's name with that of Mordred from the *Annales Cambriae*, only making Mordred Arthur's nephew rather than son. Therefore, Amr's story could be the original source for Camlann.

Our next question is what actually caused the battle? In most versions it is because Mordred tries to steal the queen and the kingdom. We have already discussed how Arthur and Mordred were holding a conference to establish peace between them when a soldier drew his sword to kill a snake and the battle accidentally began. Another early version of how the tragic battle came about is told in *The Mabinogion* tale "The Dream of Rhonabwy." The tale is told to Rhonabwy by Iddawc, the son of Mynon, who says it is his nickname which is best known. When Rhonabwy asks what Iddawc's nickname is and how he got it, he replies that it is Iddawc Cardd Prydain, and then explains its origin.

> I will tell thee the reason. I was one of the envoys at the battle of Camlan, between Arthur and Medrawd his nephew. And a spirited young man was I then! And I so craved for battle that I kindled strife between them. This was the kind of strife I kindled: when the emperor Arthur would send me to remind Medrawd that he was his foster-father and uncle, and ask for peace lest the kings' sons of

the Island of Britain and their noblemen should be slain, and when Arthur would speak to me the fairest words he could, I would speak those words the ugliest way I knew how to Medrawd. And because of that the name of Iddawg the Embroiler of Britain was set on me. And because of that was woven the battle of Camlan. But even so, three nights before the end of the battle of Camlan I parted from them, and I went to Y Llech Las in Prydein to do penance. And I was there seven years doing penance, and I won pardon. (Jones, *Mabinogion*, 140)

It is interesting that here Arthur is called Mordred's foster-father and uncle; perhaps this statement was the earliest suggestion that Arthur was a type of father to Mordred which made this idea popular with the romancers. In either case, Arthur and Mordred are seen as trying to avoid battle, but either through fate or treachery, it could not be prevented.

Joan Wolf has given an interesting theory about the Battle of Camlann in her novel *The Road to Avalon*. This theory is certainly the result of a twentieth-century mind. Here it is Agravaine, and not Mordred, who is responsible for the battle. Agravaine has homosexual tendencies and is in love with Bedwyr, but Bedwyr loves Guinevere. Agravaine decides that if he cannot have Bedwyr, then no one will, so he plans the surprise visit to Guinevere's bedroom when she is with Bedwyr. When Guinevere is accused of adultery, Arthur, who already knows about Guinevere and Bedwyr's affair, becomes enraged with Agravaine. Arthur's army is getting ready to join the Franks and Gauls on the continent against the Saxons, and Agravaine accompanies the army and Arthur over the channel, leaving Mordred and Guinevere as regents of Britain. Agravaine then escapes from the British army and returns with the false tale that the army was defeated, Arthur was killed, and only he has lived to tell the tale. Mordred and Guinevere believe him and make preparations for Mordred to be crowned king. Mordred, however, is a weak character, and Agravaine is using him as a pawn to get the kingdom for himself. Arthur returns to England and realizes Agravaine, not Mordred, is the traitor. He fears Agravaine will try to kill Mordred, so he sends Morgan as messenger to tell Mordred to flee from the battlefield and hide in Gaul until the kingdom is back in peace. Until this point, Arthur has planned that Mordred will be his successor, but when Arthur is wounded in battle and about to die, he orders Gawain to take Mordred to Gaul, presumably to protect him. Then he inexplicably names Constantine as his heir. Constantine is hardly mentioned earlier in the novel, and it is never stated that he is Arthur's relative.

Wolf is following tradition in making Constantine Arthur's heir; however, it is strange that Mordred and Gawain should go off to Gaul, both living after Camlann. It is even more odd that if they both lived, since they were Arthur's nearest relatives, Arthur names neither of them to be his heir, nor Gawain's brother Gaheris who is also alive.

Wolf is not the first writer who allowed Mordred to live after Camlann. In the rather bizarre *Mer des Histoires* or *Ly Myreur des Histors*, (the "Sea of Stories" or "The Mirror of History" published in 1475) Jean Des Preis dit d'Outremeuse writes that after Arthur died and went to Avalon, Lancelot captured London, executed the guilty Guinevere, and then locked Mordred up with her corpse, which out of hunger Mordred ate. Lancelot then bestowed the crown on Constantine and became a hermit. Later at the age of one-hundred-seventy-seven, Lancelot went to Paris to tell of his former exploits (Fletcher 222-3). One can easily see this author was not much interested in following history or tradition despite his book purporting to provide a history of the world.

Robert of Gloucester stated not only that Mordred died at Camlann, but that Arthur struck off Mordred's head (Fletcher 198). This death certainly sounds like Llacheu's beheading, and it may be part of the old Llacheu/Amr story. The *Annals of Margan* (circa 1235) states that Mordred was buried in the same tomb as Arthur (Fletcher 190). Perhaps here we again have a connection to Llacheu if his head were buried with Guinevere, possibly on the Isle of Man, as Norma Goodrich has suggested, and later Arthur's body was also brought there.

Still another version by Leland says it was not Arthur but Hywain who killed Mordred, and then Hywain and Arthur went to Avalon (Fletcher 225). We can assume that Hywain is a variation of Gawain's name.

A possibility which may be closest to the story's historical foundations is in the *Chronicles of Anjou*. Here, in a passage derived from Geoffrey of Monmouth, Arthur's betrayer is named Morvandus. This name is a mix between Mordred and Arvandus, the imperial prefect who betrayed Riothamus (Lacy, *Arthurian Encyclopedia*, 112). Riothamus is believed by Geoffrey Ashe and others to be the historical King Arthur. Of course, Arvandus, as an imperial prefect, is not the son or nephew of King Arthur.

Most writers will agree that Mordred probably died at Camlann despite a few obscure writers' interpretations. Guinevere and Arthur's fates seem less clear. Layamon hints that Arthur murdered Guinevere and then put a curse on her head (Goodrich, *King Arthur*, 107). Other theories include that she was dragged by wild horses, or fled to Meigle in Scotland where she may be buried, or that she entered a convent. These possibilities, of course, all rest on whether or not she was still alive at the time of the Battle of Camlann.

The most popular tradition of what happened to King Arthur is that he was carried away to Avalon by Morgan le Fay so that his wounds would heal, and some day, he will return to save Britain in its hour of greatest need. Other tales say he died and was buried with Guinevere in Glastonbury; the finding of his tomb in 1191 by the monks there would attempt to verify this statement, but the bodies and the cross with Arthur and Guinevere's names on it have been missing for centuries and scholars still debate about what if anything the monks actually found. It is likely that the incident was no more than a publicity stunt planned by King Henry II to stop the English and Welsh people from believing Arthur would return and overthrow their Norman conquerors; it may have also been a sham created by the monks to please Henry II and convince him to give them patronage.

Some writers say Arthur is sleeping with his knights in a cave until Britain's hour of greatest need, at which time he will return. Yet another version, which Julian del Castillo of Spain first reported in 1582, is that Arthur was turned into a crow. This may have been the source Cervantes used when he mentioned in *Don Quixote* that Arthur had been turned into a raven (Westwood 8). The raven story may have some connection to the mysterious presence of the ravens at the Tower of London; legend says that if the ravens ever leave the Tower of London, the White Tower will fall and the power of Britain will wane (Westwood 160). Arthur is, then, perhaps a similar protector as Bran's head was said to be when it was buried at the Tower of London.

Perhaps one of the most interesting versions for our study of what happened to Arthur after Camlann exists in an anonymous short chronicle from the time of King Edward II (r.1307-27) where it states Arthur lived ten years after returning to England and winning back his kingdom from Mordred. When Arthur died, he was buried, like Uther, at Glastonbury (Fletcher 199). In the tales of his earliest sons, Gwydre, Amr, and Llacheu, Arthur also outlives each of them; if these sons were predecessors for the character of Mordred, then it seems reasonable that Arthur outlived Mordred, if Mordred were Arthur's son. Perhaps the tragedy of Camlann was simply written as a tragedy to make the end of the Arthurian legends more interesting rather than stating that Camlann or whatever kind of conflict existed, was a victory for Arthur.

However, the consistency of retellings in which Arthur dies at Camlann point to Camlann as having been a tragic battle rather than a victory. Camlann is an interesting and exciting moment in Arthurian literature particularly because it is when Arthur is slain by his own son. If Camlann did not result in such a tragedy, it would have merely been one more of Arthur's many triumphant battles. All the knights, love affairs, and victorious battles that make Arthur's story great would fail to hold our interest if we did not know it was all to result in a tragic end. If Arthur were not great, his stories would not have been remembered, and what makes him most memorable is his tragic end. Furthermore, the earliest source for

Camlann states that Arthur and Mordred both died there, so any version that says differently is not faithful to tradition.

Finally, Gervase writes that Arthur was once discovered by a Sicilian groom, and Arthur told him he has been lying there ever since the battle with Mordred, his wounds annually reopening (Loomis, *Wales*, 71). Perhaps this depiction goes back to Celtic mythology also, and Arthur is acting out a part here as a relative to the Fisher King since both Arthur and the Fisher King are mythological descendants of Bran. (To understand fully Arthur's Fisher King connections, I refer the reader to Helaine Newstead's *Bran the Blessed in Arthurian Romance*).

What also reminds us of Celtic mythology is that Arthur's wounds reopen annually. It is almost as if Arthur has to fight Mordred once again every year, an annual tradition that may go back to the Welsh tale where Gwythyr and the god Gwynn must fight every May 1st until Judgment Day for the maiden Kreiddylat. Otherwise, the reopening of the wounds may represent the continual passing from one year to the next as May 1st represented the return of summer after winter for the Celtic peoples.

Whatever happened at the Battle of Camlann, nearly all sources are in agreement that Mordred fought Arthur for the kingship of Britain. What we now need to consider is the truth of all the evidence that depicts Mordred as a traitor. Scotland has a tradition that Arthur, rather than Mordred, was the one at fault, and so it is now to Scotland we will look for an alternative version of the Arthurian legend.

Chapter 9: Mordred, Scotland's Beloved King

King Arthur varies from a positive to a negative figure in the various Scottish chronicles. Since the sources for these chronicles are often not known, it is impossible to determine whether any truth is contained in the Scottish treatments of King Arthur. Our extant copies of histories from Scotland that deal with King Arthur only date from the fourteenth century or later, nearly nine hundred years after King Arthur's death so their validity is questionable. The Scottish histories' original source may be *The Northern Annals*, which contained much of early Scottish history; however, this chronicle was lost in Scotland in the thirteenth century and has not yet been recovered (Goodrich, *Guinevere*, 128). Since a century long gap exists between the loss of this document and the earliest written Scottish history that mentions King Arthur, we have further reason to question the accuracy of these histories. Another possible source for these histories was the list containing the names of the early Scottish and Pictish Kings; this list has not been seen since it disappeared from Holyrood Castle, Edinburgh in 1660, and we cannot be sure if it actually did contain information that would be useful in our study. Also King Edward I of England, when at war with Scotland, removed many documents from Scotland. These records have been lost to posterity, and probably, they were destroyed during Edward I's reign (Goodrich, *Guinevere*, 128). Perhaps these documents would have given us information necessary to piecing together the historical biographies of Arthur, Mordred, and Guinevere, but because we can only guess at what these documents contained, we cannot be certain if what was written in Scotland about King Arthur after the thirteenth century was owing to a historical tradition or merely to Scottish nationalism.

Furthemore, these documents were still extant during most medieval Arthurian writers' lifetimes, so it is strange that none of the medieval writers were familiar with the documents' contents if they contained information about King Arthur. These writers may have simply chosen to ignore the Scottish traditions of King Arthur, or more likely, the Scottish traditions were not in these lost documents, but only came into existence after the thirteenth century.

Scotland's negative view of King Arthur may largely be the result of Geoffrey of Monmouth's writings. In *The History of the Kings of Britain*, Arthur conquers Scotland, and later, it is the treacherous Scot Mordred by whom Arthur falls. However, Geoffrey cannot be accused of having a bias against Scotland, as Lacy points out, for Arthur does have some important Scottish allies in Geoffrey's book (Lacy, *Arthurian Encyclopedia*, 495).

The Scots particularly disliked King Arthur because of Merlin's prophecies in *The History of the Kings of Britain* that Arthur is the king who will come again and hold all of Britain. The English, particularly King Edward I (r. 1272-1307), chose to interpret this statement to mean England had a legitimate claim to rule over Scotland (Goodrich, *King Arthur*, 333). Parry and Caldwell point out that Edward I, when disputing with Pope Boniface VIII over the sovereignity of Scotland, even cited Geoffrey of Monmouth's narrative, with the approval of his barons, as proof of his claim to Scotland (Loomis, *Arthurian Literature*, 88).

The Scots were also upset that a Scot, Mordred, would be held responsible for Arthur's downfall. They said that Arthur was the actual traitor against Mordred because he, not Arthur, was the rightful king of Britain.

In the Vatican is a version of Geoffrey's *The History of the Kings of Britain* which states that Arthur was not even of royal birth, and Arthur's position as a leader was due chiefly to his preeminent ability (Fletcher 28-9). Arthur could be royal if his parents were of royal blood, but it is not until Geoffrey of Monmouth that Uther appears as Arthur's father (Fletcher 59). Even then, Uther is only Arthur's father because the phrase in Nennius of "Arthur mab Uter" was mistranslated to mean "Arthur, son of Uther," but more likely it may have meant "Arthur the Terrible" or "terrible warrior" (Fletcher 89). Although Arthur has sons and nephews in the Welsh tradition, who do not appear in Geoffrey, no genealogy exists for him in Welsh tradition (Bromwich, *Arthur Welsh*, 110).

The Scottish chroniclers, although they usually credit Arthur as being Igraine and Uther's son, argue that Arthur was illegitimate because he was conceived before his parents were married. It is his sister Anna, conceived and born in wedlock, whom the succession should have passed through, making her sons, Mordred and Gawain, the rightful heirs to the throne. One Scottish chronicle that argues for Arthur's illegitimacy is John of Fordun's *Chronica Gentis Scotorum* (1385); this work also takes great pains to dispute the romancers and show Mordred was of legitimate birth (Fletcher 242; Lacy, *Arthurian Encylopedia*, 496). Fletcher believes Fordun's history is from current traditions of Scotland built up by Geoffrey of Monmouth's sections on Scotland with occasional hints from Bede (243). Another Scottish work to argue for Arthur's illegitimacy is George Buchanan's *Rerum Scoticarum Historia* (1582), which says Merlin and Uther invented the tale of Arthur's birth to lessen Igerne's shame (Lacy, *Arthurian Encyclopedia*, 498).

In these sources, Arthur becomes king only as regent since Uther died while Anna's sons were still children. It was deemed necessary for Arthur to rule the kingdom and protect it against the Saxons until Anna's sons grew to be men (Fletcher 242; Lacy, *Arthurian Encyclopedia*, 496). However, this statement does not explain why Anna's husband could not have been regent until his and Anna's sons were old enough to govern the kingdom.

Another Scottish history tells a slightly different version. In Hector Boece's *Scotorum Historia* (1527), Loth the King of the Picts is married to Aurelius Ambrosius' elder sister. It is Uther who refuses to acknowledge Mordred as his rightful successor, which leads to wars between the Picts and Britain. Peace is restored after Uther's death when Arthur recognizes Mordred as his future successor. Arthur's barons, however, persuade Arthur to annul this agreement, causing Mordred to renew hostilities. The two kings are both killed at a battle on the Humber. Mordred's ally, King

Eugenius of Scotland, becomes master of the field and takes Queen Guinevere as his prisoner; she then remains a prisoner in Scotland until her death when she is buried at Meigle (W. Stewart 209-261).

Goodrich, citing Boece, says that when Guinevere was taken prisoner by the Picts, she was more likely welcomed home by them, and they were so happy to have her back that they built a monument to her. This information would help to explain Goodrich's theory that Guinevere was originally kidnapped by Arthur so he could possess her land (*Guinevere* 217). However, it is doubtful that Arthur would have kidnapped Guinevere, or that she was a virginal queen as Goodrich wants to argue, so we should be skeptical of this idea. However, if Guinevere and Mordred were both from Scotland, it might help explain why she would have been Mordred's accomplice in treason against King Arthur.

At least one Scottish work, George Buchanan's *Rerum Scoticarum Historia* (1582) admits that Guinevere plotted with Mordred for Arthur's downfall (Lacy, *Arthurian Encyclopedia*, 498). If Guinevere had been kidnapped from Scotland by Arthur, who can blame her for wanting to help her countryman, Mordred, against their mutual enemy?

We could theorize that the Scots were merely trying to rewrite history to increase Scottish nationalism and to destroy England's claim of a right to rule Scotland. However, we get hints from other non-Scottish sources that the Scottish versions may very well be the true ones. Perhaps those writers supporting Scottish nationalism were creating a tradition that already existed although they were unaware of it; therefore, both ideas are possibly correct.

One statement we cannot forget is the Welsh assertion that one of the reasons for the Battle of Camlann was not the blow Mordred struck Arthur, but rather the blow Arthur struck Mordred (Guest, *Mabinogion*, 343). We do not know whether Arthur had just cause for striking Mordred, but it seems strange that if the Welsh had so many good things to say about Mordred, as we have seen in Chapter 5, that such a sudden change would occur in his character without any explanation.

Fletcher points out that Gildas' twenty-three brothers resisted Arthur while Gildas was in Ireland. Since Gildas was not in Britain at the time, perhaps it explains why he was not familiar enough with Arthur to mention him in his book (Fletcher 105). That Gildas' brothers had to resist Arthur might suggest that Arthur was trying to conquer the land and usurp the throne, but it could also mean that Gildas' brothers were merely on the side of the kings who rebelled against Arthur as their rightful king.

In Layamon's *Brut*, we find Mordred promising the people of Winchester "free law" for evermore if they will fight on his side against Arthur. Later, Arthur arrives in Winchester and hangs its people (Fletcher 155), most likely for treason; however, it may have been wiser if Arthur had won them over to his side by granting them clemency. Certainly, Arthur looks like more of a tyrant here than does Mordred.

One of the most prejudicial statements made against the Scottish is in the *Chronicle of Scotland in a Part*, or *The Scottis Originale*. Here Arthur is definitely a tyrant, and Mordred and Gawain, the true heirs to the throne of Britain, are passed over because they are Scottish (Lacy, *Arthurian Encyclopedia*, 496).

William Stewart, at the request of Scotland's King James V, translated Boece's history into verse in 1535, adding to it considerably. In his work, he calls Arthur the most unfortunate of all British kings, one who was punished by God for being "faithless and untrue" to King Mordred (Lacy, *Arthurian Encyclopedia*, 497).

It seems doubtful that this tradition of Mordred as rightful king over Arthur was around before Geoffrey of Monmouth. However, we cannot help noticing that Geoffrey was sloppy about tying up all of his loose ends, mainly in the case of Merlin's prophecy concerning Uther's descendants. In *The History of the Kings of Britain*, a star appears three times in the sky; Merlin tells Uther the star is a sign that Uther's brother, Aurelius Ambrosius, has died and now Uther is High King. Merlin continues to prophesy as follows:

> The beam of light, which stretches from the shore of Gaul, signifies your son, who will be a most powerful man. His dominion shall extend over all the kingdoms which the

beam covers. The second ray signifies your daughter, whose sons and grandsons shall hold one after the other the kingship of Britain. (201)

Layamon expands this version by stating that Uther's daughter will have seven fair sons "who will win to their own hands many a kingdom" (Layamon 165-6).

It seems strange that Geoffrey should have included this prophecy in his work if he did not plan to have it fulfilled. If the version of the legend coming out of Scotland is true, however, then at least one of Anna's sons, Mordred, briefly held the kingship of Britain. However, the prophecy says Anna's grandsons will also hold the kingship. Gawain is credited with having children, but they are only briefly mentioned. The only son of Anna who had children was Mordred, as we are first told in Geoffrey's *The History of the Kings of Britain* and his *Vita Merlini*, and these sons at least tried to hold the kingship of Britain.

We do not know whether the prophecies Geoffrey credits to Merlin are of his own invention, or whether they were borrowed from the ancient book he claims to have used as his source, but which most scholars believe never existed. Mordred's two sons appear for the first time in Geoffrey of Monmouth's writing so that we must be skeptical of their historical reality; however, if Mordred's sons did have some sort of historical basis, and if Merlin's prophecy reflected something close to an ancient tradition about the kings of Britain, perhaps we can arrive at a conclusion that will show the Scottish traditions concerning Mordred had some validity.

Chapter 10: Mordred's Sons

To discuss Mordred's sons, we must also discuss Constantine, since the only time the sons of Mordred are mentioned in either Geoffrey's *The History of the Kings of Britain* or in his *Vita Merlini* is in context with Constantine; the fates of these three would-be kings are eternally linked together. In the *Vita Merlini*, Geoffrey states that each of Mordred's two sons, after the Battle of Camlann, desired to conquer the kingdom for himself and began to wage war, slaying all those who were kin to them. Then Constantine went to war with Mordred's sons and destroyed the people and cities until he killed the royal princes. He was then crowned and ruled over the people of Britain (97). Geoffrey is even more detailed in his *History*:

> As soon as Constantine had been crowned, the Saxons and the two sons of Mordred promptly rose against him. They failed in their attempt to overthrow him; and, after a long series of battles, they fled. One of them made his way into London and the other to Winchester, and they took command of those two cities....Constantine continued to harass the sons of Mordred. First he forced the Saxons to submit to his authority; and then he captured the two cities which I have mentioned. He killed one of the young men in front of the altar in the church of St. Amphibalus, where he was taking refuge. The second hid himself in the monastery of certain friars in London. Constantine discovered him and slew him without mercy, beside the altar there. (262)

With the exception of Geoffrey, few writers have paid attention to Mordred's sons. They are only known to have appeared in three other sources during the Middle Ages. The first of these is in

Layamon, where one of them is given the name Meleon; Fletcher points out that this name is also shared by a hero in one of the old French lays (158). Layamon, however, seems to have been in the habit of creating names for characters who previously did not have them, so this name is probably his own invention. Again in the French *Mort Artu*, one of the sons is given a name (Bruce, *Evolution*, vol. 1, 31). In some medieval works, Meleon is spelled as Melehan and according to some Internet sources, at least one work gives the brother's name as Melou, although what work provides this name is not given. These website sources I found appear unreliable, although both these names appear in the recent novel *Camelot Lost* (2008) by Jessica Bonito.

A slightly different tradition concerning Mordred's sons is in Walter Map's *La Mort al roi Artu* in which Mordred's sons make themselves the masters of the kingdom. However, in this work Lancelot and his kinsman, rather than Constantine, slay Mordred's sons, and the work does not state who ruled England after Mordred's sons (Bruce, *Evolution*, vol. 2, 378). Another version where Lancelot defeats Mordred's two sons is in the stanzaic *Le Morte D'Arthur*, written around 1460-80 (Lacy, *Arthurian Encyclopedia*, 526).

The disagreement over who slew Mordred's sons may not be a major issue, however, compared to determining whether any historical truth exists behind their existence. No known Welsh tradition exists for Mordred's sons. They seem to be the invention of Geoffrey of Monmouth, the idea for which he found in Gildas. As we have seen, Gildas never mentions King Arthur in his work, but he subjects Constantine to a lengthy attack for his sins. Among the charges Gildas makes against Constantine is that Constantine disguised himself in the habit of a holy abbot among the sacred altars, and then he, with sword and javelin, murdered the two royal youths with their attendants while their arms were stretched out toward God and his altar (Gildas 314). Gildas gives no mention of whom these royal youths are, which left Geoffrey free to adopt them as Mordred's sons. Geoffrey also exaggerated the importance of

Constantine, who is the King of Dumnonia, by making him Arthur's successor, which he never was in earlier traditions (Ashe 131).

Of course, if Mordred did have sons, these sons would have had a mother. After our long discussion of Mordred's possible abduction of Guinevere, we can assume that if she did bear Arthur children, she could have also been the mother to Mordred's sons, but only the *Alliterative Morte Arthure* concludes that Guinevere was the mother of Mordred's sons (Lacy, *Arthurian Encyclopedia*, 262). That more of the chroniclers did not reach this conclusion might be the result of Mordred's sons being largely ignored or forgotten, and even more probably because it was too ghastly a thought for Guinevere to bear Mordred's children. Furthermore, although Guinevere is the mother of at least Llacheu in Welsh tradition, Geoffrey of Monmouth seems also to be the one who invented Guinevere's barrenness; he may have done so to prevent readers from assuming that Guinevere was the mother of Mordred's sons.

However, the argument of Guinevere's barrenness is not the strongest for why she cannot be the mother of these sons. After all the connections we have made to show Llacheu, Amr, and Gwydre as predecessors of Mordred, and if Llacheu were Guinevere's son, and Mordred is a later version of Llacheu, it would almost be as if the original legends were being perverted so that the son could beget children upon his mother. It would also be as unlikely for Mordred and Guinevere to have been brother and sister as already suggested (Fletcher 141).

The best argument for why Guinevere could not be the mother of Mordred's sons is simply the time in which we must place them. We have no source stating that Guinevere and Mordred had children, and even if they did, the only opportunity they would have had for conceiving a child would be when they were left as regents of the kingdom while Arthur was on the continent. The amount of time they served as regents before Arthur's return could not have been long, but if we surmise it was a year between the time Arthur left England and the time of the Battle of Camlann, Guinevere would have had time to bear only one child, unless she had twins.

If Mordred's sons were born around the time of the Battle of Camlann, then they would have been only infants when Constantine succeeded Arthur. Since the slaying of Mordred's sons and the fighting with his own nephew are the only things Geoffrey relates as happening to Constantine during his reign, we can assume that Constantine's reign was a short one. It is doubtful that Mordred's sons would have grown up and then have carried arms against Constantine. It sounds as if Constantine fought Mordred's sons soon after the Battle of Camlann. Obviously, he could not have fought them, nor could they have been bearing arms against him, if they were toddlers. Therefore, it is both unlikely that these sons were born at the time of Camlann, or that Guinevere was their mother.

King Arthur is usually portrayed as a teenager when he pulls the sword from the stone. It is unlikely Mordred's sons could have carried arms or led armies against Constantine before their teen or at least pre-teen years. If the Battle of Camlann were fought around 539 A.D., we can assume then that Mordred's sons were born no later than the 520s.

Arthur seems to have been born around 475 A.D. Mordred is generally conceived shortly after Arthur becomes king, say 490-495, which would make Mordred a middle-aged adult at the time of Camlann, and certainly old enough to have teenagers or even grown men for sons. If by the 520s, Mordred had been acknowledged as heir to the kingdom, which he undoubtedly was if Arthur trusted him enough to leave him as regent, Mordred probably would have made an arranged dynastic marriage.

One wife whom Mordred is credited with having is named in Boece's *History and Chronicles of Scotland* (1527). Here it states that Mordred was betrothed to Gawolane's daughter because Mordred was the greatest of the Northern princes of Britain. Boece's Gawolane is Sir Gawain, and he is described as Mordred's "Gude-father," a term meaning father-in-law (W. Stewart 238). It may seem strange to us that Mordred should marry his half-brother's daughter, but as we have stated earlier, uncles marrying their nieces were not uncommon. Furthermore, Mordred claimed the kingdom of Pictland as Loth's son, meaning he must be the eldest of Loth's children; in fact, Gawain is the only other one of Loth's sons mentioned. However, Mordred is often not Loth but Arthur's son. Since Loth is often one of Arthur's enemies, a marriage to Loth's granddaughter would have better cemented his claim to the throne of Pictland. Mordred would have needed to better his claim to Pictland's throne if he were going to admit to being Arthur's son; then, he would not be Loth's son so he would have no claim to Loth's throne. It is strange that Mordred would even have a claim to Loth's throne since, in most versions of the legend, Mordred is the youngest of the five princes of Orkney.

Another possible wife for Mordred may be found if we recall our earlier discussion of the Battle of Camlann. Crawford and Johnson made the strange statement that Arthur was killed by a Mordred who was Vortigern's granddaughter's husband (Goodrich, *Merlin*, 91). Mordred may have married a descendant of Vortigern and then tried to claim the right to rule Britain because of this marriage since Vortigern had been High King before Aurelius Ambrosius. The Saxons would have probably been more willing to follow someone allied to Vortigern's house, since they had once been Vortigern's allies, than someone who was a member of Arthur's family. By marrying a descendant of Vortigern, Mordred would have united the two royal houses of Britain.

Another possibility no scholar has suggested before may exist in Mordred's friendship and later alliance with the Saxons. The most frequently accepted date for the Battle of Mount Badon is 516. This date is not many years before the probable date for the birth of Mordred's sons in the 520s. The Battle of Mount Badon generally marks the end of Arthur's wars with the Saxons. After the Saxons are defeated at Mount Badon, they become Arthur's sworn subjects and allies. One of the Saxon chiefs, Cerdic, was reputedly granted Hampshire and Somerset by Arthur when he took his oath of allegiance (Fletcher 186). What better way to be sure of Saxon loyalty to Arthur than to have Arthur's son and heir marry a Saxon woman of high rank?

If Mordred had married a Saxon, it would have strengthened the Briton and Saxon alliance, or at least have been a means of peace between the two peoples. Such a marriage would also explain why the Saxons fought on Mordred's side at the Battle of Camlann. In the chronicles of the Angles, we are told that Mordred, wishing to reign, but fearing Cerdic alone, gave Cerdic certain districts; Cerdic was then crowned at Winchester while Mordred was crowned at London (Fletcher 186). Strangely enough, these two cities are where Mordred's sons flee and are murdered by Constantine. Perhaps these were the capitals of their father and Saxon grandfather's kingdoms.

It is unlikely the Saxons would have fought for any British king without hope for personal gain. If Mordred were married to one of their own women, then his children, who would be half-Saxon, would someday inherit the kingdom; therefore, the Saxon peoples may have anticipated that the Battle of Camlann would be the battle to end all battles and would gain their people equal status to the natives of Britain.

If Mordred did have sons, these sons would have been King Arthur's direct heirs after their father, and therefore, upon Arthur and Mordred's deaths, one of them should have been named king of Britain. However, it is always Constantine whom Arthur names as his heir. Arthur may have purposely overlooked his own grandsons as his heirs because they were of Saxon blood and had fought on their father's side at Camlann. Furthermore, the people of Britain probably would not have accepted a Saxon, even if he were half-British, to rule over them, and Arthur would have been aware of this resistance. Mordred's other four brothers seem to have all died either when fighting against Lancelot or at the Battle of Camlann, so Arthur could not have named one of them as his successor. Therefore, Constantine, as Arthur's nearest loyal relative, should have inherited the throne. But how was Constantine related to Arthur, and just how legitimate was his claim to the throne if Mordred's sons still lived? It is to Constantine we must now turn to find an answer to why none of Arthur's descendants inherited the throne of Britain.

Chapter 11: Constantine

Constantine is the son of Cador, Duke of Cornwall, at least in most versions of the Arthurian legend, and Cador and Arthur are always said to be related. However, since the exact relationship between Arthur and Constantine is never really clear, perhaps Arthur and Constantine were never actually related at all. Rhys believes that Geoffrey of Monmouth simply decided he would take the kings listed in Gildas and have them succeed each other; hence, Constantine succeeds Arthur, followed by Aurelius Conan, Vortiporius, and Malgo (Rhys 17). This borrowing by Geoffrey is possible since we cannot prove that any of these kings ever ruled over all of Britain, and we already suspect that Geoffrey borrowed from Gildas to create the two sons of Mordred.

Another possibility, not referring to a blood relationship, for the reason why Arthur named Constantine as his heir, may be found in the *Life of St. Carannog.* Here it states that on the coast of Somerset, opposite Wales, Arthur reigned as co-prince with Cato, or Cadwy. This other ruler later appeared in the romances as Cador (Lacy, *Arthurian Handbook*, 25). If Arthur were without an heir, and if Cador died before him, so that Constantine was co-ruler when Arthur died, it seems reasonable that Arthur would give Constantine the entire kingdom.

Most writers, however, state that Constantine was Arthur's relative, and some even say he was Arthur's nephew. Of course, these statements could have been created to explain why the kingdom passed from Arthur to Constantine if the above reason were not known by the chroniclers.

If Constantine were related to Arthur, it is undoubtedly through his father, Cador. According to Geoffrey's *The History of the Kings of Britain*, a Cador Limenich fell at Camlann. Norma Goodrich assumes that this person was Cador, Constantine's father (*King Arthur* 97), and with his death, Constantine then became the nearest loyal relative to King Arthur. It is then Cador's relation to Arthur that we must determine in order to understand Constantine's right to Arthur's throne.

Geoffrey of Monmouth refers to Constantine as Arthur's cousin in *The History of the Kings of Britain* (261). In the *Vita Merlini*, Geoffrey calls Constantine Arthur's nephew (97). Layamon and Wace, although they closely follow Geoffrey, are less specific in the relation. Layamon has Arthur address Cador, "Cador, thou art mine own kin" (197), but this kinship as we shall see may be as an in-law rather than through blood. In Wace, it is only at Arthur's death that any mention occurs of their being related, at which point Arthur gives his crown to Constantine, whom Arthur addresses as "his near kin" (114). Although Cador and Constantine occasionally occur elsewhere in these and other chronicles, it is usually not until the end of these works that this relationship is mentioned.

Among the theories of how Cador and Arthur are related is that they are both members of Igraine's family. In "Culwch and Olwen," Igraine has four brothers and two sisters. Cador could be one of these brothers or the son of one of Igraine's siblings, which would make either him or Constantine Arthur's cousin. However, this same story also gives Arthur a half-brother named Ricca (Blaess 72). Ivor Arnold has suggested that Cador was the son of Igraine and Gorlois (Blaess 71). Possibly, Cador and Ricca is the same person, and therefore, Cador is Arthur's half-brother, making Constantine King Arthur's nephew. This form of relation also appears in John Hardyng's *Chronicle* (1436), where Cador is Arthur's brother on his mother's side, and Constantine is definitely represented as Arthur's nephew (Fletcher 251). This theory would help explain why Cador was Duke of Cornwall since he would have inherited the dukedom from his father, Gorlois, but other theories still exist about Arthur and Constantine's relationship.

Blaess points out that in the Vulgate Arthurian Romances, Igraine has two husbands before Uther. By her first unnamed husband, Igraine had two daughters, and then Igraine had three daughters by her second husband, Gorlois, Duke of Cornwall. The oldest unnamed girl married Lot, by whom she had five sons. Of Igraine's other four daughters, one could have been Cador's mother, or one could have married Cador and then been the mother of Constantine (76). However, a child fathered by Igraine's first husband would not receive its stepfather's title of Duke of Cornwall, so it is by Igraine and Gorlois then that Cador and Constantine must be related to Arthur.

The *Brut Tysillio* states directly that Cador, Constantine's father, was the son of Gorlois. Fletcher remarks that this statement could be part of an old British tradition, but more likely, the author was borrowing from Geoffrey of Monmouth and elaborating on some of Geoffrey's statements as he went along (118). One modern writer who has tried to clarify this confusion is Persia Woolley; in her novel *Child of the Northern Spring* (1987), she makes Cador the son of Gorlois by his first marriage rather than by Igraine (141). This relationship seems possible since Gorlois is often depicted as an old man at the time of his marriage to the young Igraine. By Igraine, Gorlois then becomes the father of Morgan and Morgause. Arthur then becomes a stepbrother to Cador.

Woolley also reinterprets the confusion caused by Mark and Gorlois both being in Cornwall. She makes Mark the King of Cornwall, and then Gorlois, since he is never more than a duke, is the vassal to Mark. By placing Mark and Gorlois in different hierarchial positions, it becomes clear that no blood relationship exists between Mark and Gorlois. This clarification, however, is inaccurate if, as Geoffrey of Monmouth frequently states, Cador is King of Cornwall (227); however, Geoffrey seems to have been in the habit of interchanging the titles of duke and king, as when he refers to Arthur's nephew Hoel sometimes as a king and sometimes as a duke. Lacy has suggested that at the time Gildas writes, Britain had broken into small kingdoms and Constantine was the ruler of Dumnonia, a territory that comprised Cornwall, Devon, Somerset and some, but not much, territory beyond. Constantine's enlargement into Arthur's cousin and successor reflects the belief, current before Geoffrey of Monmouth, and perhaps factually based, that Arthur's home country was in this region (Lacy, *Arthurian Handbook*, 330).

If Cador is merely Arthur's stepbrother, there really is no blood relation; therefore, Cador and his son would have no real claim to the throne of Britain, an interesting possibility I will discuss further below.

Another possibility is that Cador is the son of one of Arthur's unnamed sisters. This possibility would work if Arthur had no half-brother or stepbrother to inherit the Duchy of Cornwall, so that it would pass through a sister. Several romances take up the idea of an unnamed sister of Arthur as the mother of Cador, such as the *Morte Arthure*, Malory's *Le Morte D'Arthur*, *Syre Gawene and the Carle of Carelyle*, *The Awntyrs of Arthur at the Terne Wathelyne*, *Arthur*, *Merlin*, and *Golagrus and Gawain* (Blaess 76). Most likely, since Cador becomes Duke of Cornwall, his mother, Arthur's unnamed sister, is the daughter of Gorlois, and may or may not be the daughter of Igraine.

Another possibility is that Cador is somehow related to Uther. If he were the child of Uther and Igraine's daughter, then Constantine, by becoming king, and his nephew after him, would fulfill Merlin's prophecy in *The History of the Kings of Britain* that Anna would have sons who would rule as kings. However, not even the slightest hint exists here that Cador is in any way related to Anna. Still it would seem that if Constantine were Arthur's relative, it should be on his father's side since Uther's father was also named Constantine, so Cador's son may have been named after his ancestor. Perhaps Cador was an illegitimate child of Uther before his marriage to Igraine; considering the tradition of Uther's fondness for women, this illegitimacy could be a possibility. The best argument for Constantine's relation to Uther is that Arthur inherited his throne from his father, rather than his mother; therefore, one of Uther's rather than Igraine's relatives would be heir to the throne. Igraine was not a member of the royal Roman line to which Uther belonged; therefore, no relative of hers would have a legitimate claim to being king. If Cador were Uther's relative, however, it would not explain why he was Duke of Cornwall, unless Uther granted him the dukedom after the death of Gorlois.

Another possible connection that would make Constantine a relative of Arthur exists in Arthur's marriage to Guinevere. This connection also originates in *The History of the Kings of Britain*, when Geoffrey states that Guinevere was brought up in Cador, Duke of Cornwall's household (221). Later writers seem to have interpreted this statement to mean that Cador was Guinevere's guardian and probably also her relative. Wace states that Guinevere was "the earl's near cousin, for by his mother, he, too, was of Roman blood," and Guinevere is also described as being from a noble Roman house (53-4). If Wace is correct, Cador's mother could be Arthur's sister either by Gorlois or Uther, since they are both Roman.

Layamon writes of Guinevere "This maiden's mother was of Romanish men, Cador's relative" (204). In Sir Thomas Gray's *Scalacronica* (1355), Guinevere is cousin to Cador of Cornwall and daughter to the King of Biscay (Fletcher 225), and in John Stow's *The Chronicles of England* (1580), she is again Cador's cousin and the King of Biscay's daughter. Parke Godwin's novel *Firelord* (1980) finally does make Prince Cador the father of Guinevere, and therefore, Cador is Arthur's father-in-law.

It is also possible that Arthur was already related to Cador, so when he married Guinevere, he was marrying his own cousin to some degree, although none of the writers go so far as to state that any blood relation existed between Arthur and Guinevere. It is more likely then, that through his marriage, Arthur gained Cador as an in-law. Still a relationship to Cador through Guinevere does not make sense, unless a blood relationship existed between Arthur and Guinevere, since Cador would still not be Arthur's blood relative; therefore, his son would have no right to the throne. Even the statements that Guinevere was of Roman blood do not make sense if we follow the opinions of Norma Goodrich and some other scholars that she was probably Celtic or Pictish. However, since

Geoffrey is the first one to state Guinevere's family origins, Norma Goodrich's theories seem less likely than what Geoffrey stated to be the case.

After the Battle of Camlann, Arthur may have had no other living male blood relatives other than Mordred's sons, so he would have had no choice but to designate a successor allied to his family through marriage. It is true that Arthur is given other nephews such as Hoel and Owain, but they are generally forgotten in the literary works after Geoffrey's time, and we may even assume that they were already dead or died at Camlann. Whether or not Constantine was a blood relative, he was probably the closest to an heir Arthur had after Mordred and Mordred's two sons. Therefore, Constantine was rightful heir, but despite that degree of importance, the first written mention of him is in Gildas, where he is given a blackened character. Gildas definitely does not see Constantine's murder of the two royal youths as righteous, no matter how Geoffrey rewrites it, and since Gildas was historically closer to the Arthurian period, let us just assume for a moment that Constantine did wrongfully slay Mordred's sons.

To take such a viewpoint, we have to go back to events that make little if any sense if we ask some "what if" questions. First, what if Cador is the son of Gorlois by an earlier marriage? Morgan and Morgause are often depicted as hating Arthur because they blame Uther for murdering Gorlois, since he was their father. Arthur at least shares the blood of his mother with these two half-sisters, but in this case, Cador would be a step-brother and have absolutely no reason to love Arthur if Arthur's father killed his own father. Then let us ask what if Mordred had not revolted against Arthur so that Arthur died naturally of old age? Who then would have succeeded Arthur as King of Britain? Since Mordred is Arthur's son, or at least nephew, he probably would have been Arthur's heir. Arthur seems to have intended Mordred as his successor, or why else would he have left Mordred as regent while he went to the continent? Arthur may have felt that making Mordred regent would be good practice for the time when Mordred would be king. Joan

Wolf adopts this reason for Mordred's creation as regent in her novel *The Road to Avalon*.

If Mordred were recognized by Arthur as his successor, then he was assured of someday becoming King of Britain, so why would he try to steal his father's kingdom? Arthur must have been in his sixties by this time, and considering the time period, it is unlikely he would have lived many more years so Mordred only needed to be patient and soon he would become king.

However, suppose Mordred were impatient to be king. Would he have waited until Arthur was away, and then have had to wait for Arthur's army to return and fight him? Mordred could have saved himself a lot of trouble by finding some Saxon hitman to do away with Arthur. There could be little question of motive if a Saxon murdered Arthur, since Arthur had been the Saxons' enemy for a generation. Mordred could have easily arranged such a crime without having any suspicion directed toward him. If Mordred were the greatly honored person he is regarded as in Welsh tradition, among whose good qualities are calmness, it seems ridiculous that he would have plotted something as rash as a rebellion against Arthur.

Arthur hardly seems to be an obstacle to Mordred's gaining the throne. However, Mordred and his sons would have been an obstacle to Constantine's acquiring a crown. Constantine is definitely a minor figure until the time of Arthur's death. It is true that distant relatives were often adopted into royal families to carry on a dynasty, but Constantine's rise to prominence is so sudden that it is highly suspicious.

Consequently, the Battle of Camlann may have resulted from Constantine's treacherous intentions against both Arthur and Mordred. We have already seen examples of how the battle accidentally happened. Since Mordred dies in battle, and Arthur immediately afterward, before he could communicate with many people, there would have been few, especially if Constantine were Arthur's relative, to dispute Constantine's claim that Arthur had named him as his successor.

Once Constantine had Arthur and Mordred out of the way, he only had Mordred's sons to eliminate so he could have the throne. If Constantine had convinced his people that Mordred was the treacherous one, the extinction of Mordred's sons could not have been difficult. Until recently, history has usually been told from the conqueror's point of view. Because Constantine won the kingdom, and because neither Arthur, Mordred, nor Mordred's two sons lived to record what actually happened at Camlann, we may never know the truth about that battle.

Gildas may have been the only person brave enough to speak against the evil King Constantine. He certainly believed Constantine was at fault for murdering the two royal youths. Geoffrey tells us that after four years, Constantine was succeeded by his nephew Aurelius Conan. Constantine's short reign may have been the result of God punishing him for his sins. Wace even states that Constantine was assassinated by one of his own knights (Fletcher 144). This death would have been a proper end if Constantine were truly such an evil man.

After listing all of Constantine's sins, Gildas exclaims to Constantine, "Go to now, I reprove thee as present whom I know as yet to be in this life extant" (314). Gildas wrote this in 546, four years after the latest date of 542 for the Battle of Camlann. Since Constantine only ruled four years, perhaps he died from guilt after Gildas' denouncements. Another possibility is that writers sought to explain his short reign by inventing the reason that he died or was murdered.

However, a curious tradition exists that Constantine did not die after the four years he is credited with reigning. Rather, he renounced his crown after only four years as king. Constantine then went to preach the gospel to the Scots and Picts (Gildas 304). Perhaps he felt he could make up for the wrong he had done to the Scottish people when he betrayed their King Mordred by now preaching the gospel to them. It should not even seem strange to us that Constantine entered holy orders, even if he did not commit these evil deeds, since many of Arthur's companions, including Lancelot, entered holy orders after Arthur's passing.

Therefore, the traditional tales of Mordred's treachery may have been invented or deliberately written against him. If Mordred were already heir to Arthur's throne and therefore had no reason to try gaining it by force, the tale of Mordred's treachery at Camlann is lacking in some major details. Finally, that Gildas believes the royal youths were innocent while Constantine was a murderer points to an alternative and possibly more faithful version of what may have happened at the Battle of Camlann.

Constantine may be one of the reasons why none of King Arthur's descendants succeeded him as monarch of Britain, besides the cause of Mordred's name being blackened for nearly fifteen centuries. However, it is still possible that Arthur had descendants by one of his children other than Mordred.

Part III:
Arthur's Descendants

Chapter 12: Arthur, Cerdic, and Vortigern

In *The Discovery of King Arthur* (1985), Geoffrey Ashe, like several other Arthurian scholars, remarks that the Saxon Cerdic, with whom King Arthur often wars, and who eventually received Hampshire and Somerset from Arthur, has a British rather than a Saxon name. Cerdic's father, according to Saxon genealogies, was Elesa, which is a Saxon name, but it is doubtful that any Saxon would have given his son a British name when the Saxons warred against the British in the fifth century (198-9).

If Elesa is not Cerdic's father, then we must ask who is. Among the novelists, both Rosemary Sutcliff and Persia Woolley have made Cerdic the son of Vortigern and his Saxon wife. Geoffrey Ashe presents a more interesting, but what I believe to be a less possible, suggestion that Cerdic is King Arthur's son (198-9). Considering that Cerdic fought against Arthur, and that he is also the friend of Mordred, we may ask whether some confusion exists between Mordred and Cerdic, and even whether Cerdic is really the historical Mordred.

Ashe suggests that perhaps Vortigern married his Saxon wife, Lady Rowena, about 430. Their marriage resulted in a daughter being born. This daughter then married Arthur-Riothamus (Ashe is here arguing that Riothamus is the historical King Arthur) sometime in the 450s. Their marriage was part of the arrangement that made Arthur the High King of Britain. Their son, Cerdic, then born in the 450s, was three-quarters British and one quarter Saxon. Sometime in his early life, Cerdic went to Armorica and became the father of Cynric in the 470s. He then returned with his adult son, Cynric, in 495 and established a little domain on the Hampshire coast. His

Saxon blood allowed him to attract the Saxons to him as other Saxons trickled into the area.

Maximus
|
Vortigern = (1) Severa
= (2) Saxon wife
|
Daughter = Arthur-Riothamus
|
Cerdic
|
Wessex royalty
|
English royalty

(Ashe 199)

Ashe goes on to remark that if the Riothamus of Breton genealogy were Arthur, his alleged son Daniel would have been younger than Cerdic. Daniel was said to have become "king of the Alamanni," a Germanic people, who became involved with the Saxons and the Franks; some of the Alamanni may have immigrated to Britain. Ashe believes Daniel's kingship of the Alamanni hints that Riothamus' family dominated Germanic groups on the continent as Cerdic may have done (102). However, I do not feel that because Daniel may have done something similar to Cerdic, it means Cerdic was Arthur's son.

The dates for Riothamus seem early if he is King Arthur; Arthur could not have had Cerdic as a son as early as the 450s if we expect him still to be alive in 539 at the Battle of Camlann. It is impossible that Arthur could have been over the age of one-hundred at the time of the battle. Scholars have continually debated over when Arthur's reign took place, but they at least agree it was some time between 450-550 A.D (Lacy, *Arthurian Handbook*, 7). If Arthur were still capable of fighting in 539 at Camlann, a date in the 470s would be reasonable for his time of birth. Furthermore, Cerdic, according to the genealogies, was born around 467, meaning not only could

Cerdic not have been born in the 450s, but he could not be Arthur's son if he were several years older than Arthur. It is possible that these dating discrepancies are the result of the change from the Julian to the Gregorian calendar, combined with the laxity of medieval scribes and historians. Furthermore, by the time these statements were recorded, it was several centuries after the events took place. However, the tradition that Arthur and Cerdic were contemporaries has existed longer than Ashe's theory, so it seems unlikely Arthur could have been Cerdic's father.

Ashe also comments on the strange longevity of Cerdic's son Cynric, who came to Britain as an adult in 495 and did not die until 560, by which time he would have been in his eighties, a possible but doubtful lifespan for a warrior in fifth and sixth century Britain (208).

However, Ashe overlooks the fact that Cynric, according to the Church of Latter Day Saints' *Ancestral File*, was not Cerdic's son, but rather his grandson. Cerdic was born in 467, and he may have had a son around 493, known as Crioda, Prince of Wessex, who then became the father of Cynric, who was born around 525 (*Ancestral File*). It is true that no Crioda appears in *The Anglo-Saxon Chronicle*, yet it makes more sense that Cynric was Cerdic's grandson, and Cynric and Crioda's dates were combined than that Cerdic lived to such a ripe old age. Crioda never became King of Wessex so we can assume that he died before his father; therefore, the throne passed from grandfather to grandson. When Cerdic died in 534, Cynric would have been nineteen years old, old enough to be king over his father's subjects. Since Crioda died without making any major achievements, his name may have been forgotten by some of the chroniclers, so they placed Cynric's name in his place. Still Cerdic would have only been twenty-eight when arriving in England, and Crioda only two, unless Crioda had an older brother Cynric, who was born when Cerdic was barely into his teen years. In that case, Crioda's brother Cynric would be a teenager, and therefore old enough to bear arms in 495 when he arrived in England with his father. Perhaps this Cynric and his nephew, having the same name, were the ones who were blended into one person by the chroniclers. Since King Alfred the Great (r. 871-899) is traditionally considered the one who ordered *The Anglo-Saxon Chronicle* to be compiled, the recorders of the chronicles would have been recording events that happened four hundred years earlier, by which time much may have been lost or confused (*Anglo-Saxon Chronicle* xxviii).

If we follow Ashe's theory, Vortigern would have married a Saxon wife in the 430s so that Cerdic as his grandson could have been born in the 450s. However, the 430s seems much too early for Vortigern to marry any Saxon since 449 is the traditional date (according to *The Anglo-Saxon Chronicle*) for when the Saxons arrived in Britain and Vortigern befriended them. It is possible that Cerdic was born somewhere between 450 and 467, but not as Vortigern's grandson. If Cerdic is related to Vortigern, it would have to be as his son, as other scholars and novelists have already represented him to be.

It is therefore unlikely that Cerdic was Arthur's son, but he probably was Arthur's contemporary. We cannot then be interested in him as one of Arthur's children, yet he may still be a key figure in our search for Arthur's descendants. Since Arthur and Cerdic were contemporaries, their children would have also been contemporaries. We have already seen Mordred's great friendship with the Saxons, and especially with Cerdic. If Mordred were to have married one of Cerdic's daughters, then Cerdic could easily be the grandfather of Mordred's sons. Although Mordred's sons were both murdered by Constantine, such a connection could give us clues for why the English royal family has tried to claim descent from King Arthur, as we will explore in our next chapter.

One other possible connection, not concerning Cerdic, but rather Vortigern and Arthur, has been suggested by Holtzmann. This theory is that Arthur and Vortigern's son Vortimer was the same person. Holtzmann suggests that their names were identical because Vortimer became Arthur in Welsh pronunciation. He believed that the two could possibly be the same person since Vortimer is traditionally said to have risen up against the Saxons (Bruce, *Evolution*, vol. 1, 3-4). If as Ashe suggests, Arthur married

Vortigern's daughter, then Vortimer/Arthur would be the son-in-law of Vortigern. Perhaps Vortimer, as Vortigern's son-in-law, was simply referred to as his son. If this theory is true, then the descendants of King Arthur would include the descendants of Vortigern. However, it seems unlikely that Vortimer and Arthur were the same person since Vortimer dies fairly soon, and his career does not approach the glory with which Arthur's career is credited. Furthermore, Holtzmann made his suggestion in 1867, based on what he believed was a similarity between Arthur and Vortimer's names, a similarity that most scholars disagree with today. The only other child we know Vortigern is credited with is a son named Paschent or Pacentius, a name that does not suggest any similarity with Arthur's. Geoffrey of Monmouth relates that Pacentius fought against Aurelius Ambrosius, who is Arthur's uncle, and he tried to enlist the Germans as his allies in this conflict. Pacentius is also the one who hired Eopa to poison Aurelius (200), so it seems highly unlikely that Pacentius could be Arthur.

Therefore, any blood relationship between Arthur and Cerdic or Arthur and Vortigern seems highly unlikely. Except through possible marriages, Arthur's descendants are not interlinked with these other two British rulers. However, the English royal family is descended from Cerdic, and they claim descent from King Arthur. Since Cerdic is not Arthur's son, we must now look at other possibilities for how the English royal family could be descendants of King Arthur.

Chapter 13: Arthur and the English Royal Family

Among those who have tried to claim descent from King Arthur, the most prominent and most determined have been the monarchs of England. As we have already seen, little chance exists that any of King Arthur's children outlived him, and the only grandchildren he had were murdered by Constantine. These two grandsons could have been old enough to have had children of their own before they died, but this theory is only a surmise since no record, chronicle, or romance states they had heirs. Therefore, it is highly doubtful that King Arthur had any descendants who lived beyond the sixth century. Yet the royal family of England has claimed, at least since the time of the Plantagenets, that they are descended from King Arthur.

During the reigns of the Saxon kings in England, from the sixth century until 1066, there is no monarch known to have claimed descent from Arthur. It was not until after the Norman invasion that this idea became popular, and even then it seems to have been the result of the popularity of Geoffrey of Monmouth's *The History of the Kings of Britain*, which appeared around 1136. Geoffrey ended his chronicle with King Cadwallader, whom he states probably died around 689 (289). Cadwallader has numerous descendants living today, but he is not a descendant of King Arthur; neither is he from any records I have been able to locate an ancestor to the present royal family of Britain (although DNA research suggests the odds are that he is). Geoffrey leaves unaccounted for over four hundred years, from the time his book ends until the 1100s, except for making prophecies of what will happen. However, none of these prophecies hint that Arthur's descendants will reign over England. Since Geoffrey gives King Arthur no descendants, it is inconceivable how the Plantagenets could have claimed an Arthurian lineage.

The popularity of Geoffrey's book gave rebirth to the tales of King Arthur and made the conquered Anglo-Saxon peoples believe King Arthur would return to rescue them, a belief that might seem strange since the Anglo-Saxons had originally been Arthur's enemies; however, by the twelfth century, Celtic blood had so intermixed with Anglo-Saxon blood that nearly anyone in England could claim to have ancestors whom Arthur had been king over.

The belief that King Arthur would return might have made King Henry II fearful that the conquered people would become restless, and so as we have already seen, he may have staged the finding of Arthur's body at Glastonbury. To keep the conquered under control, the royal family decided it needed to prove its members were the rightful heirs to the throne of all Britain because of their descent from King Arthur or at least his family.

King Henry II's ancestors included the Counts of Anjou; his descent from William the Conqueror was through his mother, whereas it was his father who was Count of Anjou. However, William the Conqueror's great-grandparents included a daughter of the House of Anjou, and a Duke of Brittany, both of whom could possibly have claimed an ancestry from Arthurian times. William the Conqueror's paternal lineage from the Dukes of Normandy went back to a Scandinavian and Viking ancestry that settled in Normandy in the 800s. The House of Anjou can trace its descent back to Tertulle, Count of Anjou (born about 821), and his wife Petronilla, Countess of Anjou (born about 825), who was a granddaughter of the Holy Roman Emperor Charlemagne (*Ancestral File*). However, the House of Anjou would have to trace its ancestors back another three hundred years if it were to claim descent from King Arthur, and it is probably no longer possible to make genealogical connections for these families that stretch so far back in time.

Two possible connections can be made between the House of Anjou and the Arthurian legends. In Geoffrey of Monmouth's *The History of the Kings of Britain*, King Arthur, after making his Gallic conquests, placed his seneschal, Kay, in charge of Anjou. He also placed Bedivere in charge of Neustria, now called Normandy (225). Neither of these Knights of the Round Table was related to King Arthur, but their descendants could include the English royal family.

A closer connection between the House of Anjou, whose members are called Angevins, and the Arthurian legends is that the Angevin family were the keepers of the Grail in Arthurian romance (Bruce, *Evolution*, vol. 1, 317). Percival's father was of the Angevin family, while his mother, Blanchefleur, often known as the Widow Lady of Camelot, is believed to have been yet another sister of King Arthur (Blaess 76). This connection would make King Arthur an ancestral uncle to the House of Anjou, if indeed they were descended from the Angevin family. Percival's son Lohengrin later migrated to the continent (Goodrich, *Guinevere*, 224), and from his children, the Royal Houses of Belgium and the Netherlands are said to descend (Goodrich, *Holy Grail*, 67, 159). Therefore, England is not the only monarchy that has tried to make an Arthurian connection; the House of Anjou may be related to King Arthur through his sister.

The Kings of England would also remain as the Kings of Anjou until Henry VI's reign when the duchy would be lost to France. However, claiming an Arthurian connection by the Angevin family was not the only attempt the Plantagenets would make to establish themselves as rightful rulers of England through a lineage to Arthur. Henry II's son Geoffrey had a son named Arthur. Arthur's mother, Constance of Brittany, had named her son Arthur in defiance of his grandfather, Henry II, as a sign of Breton independence and insubordination to the rule of the Angevin and Norman house (Norgate 58). However, the name might have also been given to show the royal family's connection to King Arthur, although at this time Henry II's son Richard was heir to the throne rather than Arthur's father, Geoffrey. The Bretons' connection to the Welsh probably made Constance of Brittany see it as an honorable name, one in conflict with her father-in-law's desire to end the belief in King Arthur's return. When Richard I died, Geoffrey was already dead, but Arthur, being the son of the next oldest male child of

Henry II, should have succeeded to the throne and become King Arthur. Richard I had always favored his nephew, Arthur, over his brother John. However, on his deathbed, Richard named John as his successor, probably to show he bore John no ill will, after all the years Philip of France had been trying to set the two brothers against each other. Arthur still had a more legitimate claim to the throne, but Richard and John's mother, Eleanor of Aquitaine, who was used to getting her own way, sided with her son John (Painter 7). Furthermore, William de Briouse and William the Marshall, two of the most powerful men in England, also sided with John (Painter 7; Norgate 57). William the Marshall was fully aware of John's monstrous character, but Prince Arthur was only twelve and already obnoxious, so William the Marshall feared that when Arthur reached adulthood, he would be an even worse king than John might be (Norgate 58). This situation shows that as late as 1199, the rules of hereditary succession were still uncertain. That Arthur had a more legitimate claim than John to the throne seemed to be a less important question than which of the two would be the least unsatisfactory monarch (Norgate 57).

John succeeded to the throne, but to solidify his claim so Arthur could not depose him, he had his ruffians murder Prince Arthur. Therefore, England was deprived of the reign of another King Arthur, although this King Arthur probably would not have lived up to his namesake.

King Edward I probably tried harder than any other Plantagenet to make the Arthurian connection. As we have already seen, he believed he was the rightful ruler over Scotland, not to mention Wales, because according to Geoffrey of Monmouth, Arthur had ruled all the Island of Britain, so if he were Arthur's heir, Edward I believed he should also rule the entire island.

Edward I, like many, also believed Winchester had originally been Camelot. During his reign he had constructed a large round table, which he placed in Winchester Castle to sustain the myth of Camelot having once been there (*Le Morte D'Arthur*).

Edward III was also enchanted by the Arthurian legends. He planned to revive the knighthood of the Round Table, but instead founded the Order of the Garter. His son, Edward the Black Prince, was said to be a true believer in the Arthurian ideal and the practice of chivalry.

However, through a possible descent from the Angevins, the Plantagenets could only number themselves as collateral rather than direct Arthurian descendants, calling Arthur their ancestral uncle. It was not until the time of the Tudors that a direct claim might have been possible.

After the death of King Henry V in 1422, his widow, Catherine of France, fell in love with the Welsh prince, Owen Tudor, who claimed Arthurian descent. Their son Edmund Tudor would marry Margaret Beaufort, a member of the English royal family, and through this marriage King Henry VII was born. Henry VII, as a member of the House of Lancaster, had the Red Rose of Lancaster as his symbol. To strengthen his claim of an Arthurian descent, he had the Red Rose of Lancaster painted in the center of the Round Table at Winchester. King Henry VII also named his eldest son Arthur, but the prince died before he could become King Arthur, and so his brother instead succeeded to the throne as King Henry VIII.

Henry VIII continued the belief in a descent from King Arthur through his Tudor ancestors by having a figure of King Arthur painted on the Round Table, with Henry VIII's own face painted as that of Arthur (*Le Morte D'Arthur*). A family resemblance between the ancient and present king was the purpose, and since no one can say what King Arthur looked like, no one could deny that Henry VIII did not resemble his supposed ancestor of a thousand years before.

Queen Elizabeth I continued the Arthurian tradition in the family. Brinkley declares that "the Arthurian ancestry of Elizabeth was given especial emphasis at the time of her coronation" (Merriman 199). When Elizabeth visited Kenilworth in 1575, an Arthurian costume party and masque were held. Upon the queen's arrival, she was met by a woman dressed as Morgan le Fay, who greeted the queen as Arthur's heir (Lacy, *Encyclopedia*, 414). During the revels, a set of trumpeters signified that the men of

Arthur's day were superior to modern men. Elizabeth talked with the Lady of the Lake, and her presence allowed her to free the Lady of the Lake from the persecutions of Bruce sans Pitee. A song was also sung of Rience's demand for Arthur's beard. It is clear that these events at Kenilworth were based upon Malory's writings (Merriman 201), and the masque in Chapter 37 of Sir Walter Scott's *Kenilworth* borrows and fictionalizes from this historical event.

The Stuart dynasty's first king, James I, also tried to claim Arthurian descent. In 1610/11, during a Christmas masque *The Speeches at Prince Henry's Barriers* written by Ben Jonson and staged by Inigo Jones, James I's son, Prince Henry, took the role of Oberon, son of King Arthur and ruler of a fairy kingdom. However, after the death of Prince Henry, the Arthurian craze among the royal family began to disappear for many generations (Lacy, *Encyclopedia*, 415; *Arthurian Handbook* 171).

Still, Norris J. Lacy tells us that at least one attempt in recent years has been made to show that Queen Elizabeth II is descended from King Arthur (*Le Morte D'Arthur*). Sir Iain Moncreiffe of that Ilk, in *Royal Highness*, a study of the ancestors of the future King of England, Prince William, conveniently states that it is very probable for King Arthur to be among the warrior chieftains of fifth and sixth century Britain from whom the Royal Family is descended (Moncreiffe 12). Finally, as Geoffrey Ashe has pointed out, Prince William's middle name is Arthur, and should Prince William choose to use his middle name rather than William when he is crowned, he will be the next King Arthur (199).

Still, no direct or indisputable genealogical line connects the British royal family to King Arthur. One other possibility may exist in the theory that the King Arthur of legend is the historical Riothamus. Riothamus had a son David who then had a son Budic. This Budic lived in Britain as an exile for some time. It is possible that Budic might be an ancestor of the Tudors, and a closer look at Welsh and Breton genealogies could then give us a connection between Riothamus and the British royal family (Ashe 196).

Of course, if Cerdic is Arthur's son, as Geoffrey Ashe has also suggested, then the British royalty would also be descended from

Arthur because Cerdic was the ancestor of Alfred the Great, and through him, the British royal family. The fact that Debrett's Peerage, the official heraldic society in Britain, backed Ashe's book suggests that the British, if not the royal family itself, still wish to make this link between their present day monarch and King Arthur. If there is a link between King Arthur and Elizabeth II, it may be years, if ever, before it will be discovered or researched thoroughly enough to be convincing. It also seems unlikely that a tradition of descent that does not seem to have begun until Henry II in the twelfth century is any more than a convenient forgery. If there is a connection, it is probably through the Welsh Tudor family, and it is there that the greatest scrutiny may need to be used.

Chapter 14: Smervie and the Clan Campbell

We now come to one of the strangest traditions in regard to King Arthur's descendants. Yet if as Norma Goodrich has argued, King Arthur actually lived in Northern England or even Scotland rather than Southern England, perhaps it is not so strange. In Scotland, the Clan Campbell has preserved the curious tradition that they are descended from King Arthur. The Duke of Argyle's 1871 study of *The House of Argyll and the Collateral Branches of the Clan Campbell from the Year 420 to the Present*, assures us that of the various conjectures as to the Campbell Clan's origins:

> ...the most probable and prevalent is, that they descended from Arthur, Prince of the Silures whose heroic valor sustained the declining state of his country in the invasions of the Saxons, and who is so much celebrated by the songs of Thaleissin [sic];...he is said to have married Elizabeth, daughter of the King of France, which behoved to be Childobert, the fifth in descent from Pharamond.... (Sellar 109)

The belief in this descent can be witnessed in recent times, as Macbain, editor of *Skene's Highlanders of Scotland* (1902) and Sir Iain Moncreiffe of that Ilk's *Highland Clans* (1967) back up by stating that the name Arthur is common among the Campbells (Sellar 110).

The Campbells' descent from King Arthur is traced along the line of a supposed son of Arthur's named Smerevie or Merevie. Duncanson's *Ane Account of the Genealogie of the Campbells* gives Arthur this son. He is described as:

a great or famous person of whom diverse and strange
things are spoken in the Irish traditions; it is said that he
was born in Dumbarton on the south syde thereof, in a
place called the redd hall or in Irish Tour in Talla Dherig
that is Tower of the redd hall or red house, he was called
to his agnomen or by-name the fool of the forrest because
he was a wild undauntoned person. (Sellar 113)

Norma Goodrich has pointed out that Irish genealogists give
King Arthur a son born in Dumbarton, which she believes is also
precisely where Lancelot and Guinevere delivered Arthur from a
Saxon or Irish prison. She says this son also figures in Irish
genealogical records as Mervie or Smerlie (*Guinevere* 59).

The Duke of Argyle stated in his history of the Campbells that
Arthur's second wife was the daughter of the Frankish king, and she
bore Arthur a son called Smerviemore, meaning the Great Smervie,
who died at the age of twenty-four. Smervie did not get the throne
after his father because he preferred hunting alone in the forest,
which is how he got his nickname "Fool of the Forest." This
Smervie also married and sired his own son, which is attested to as
during the lifetime of St. Columbo "anno 570." The Annals of
Ireland give as a line of descent, Constantine, father of Ambrosius,
father of Uther (Pendragon), father of Arthur, father of Smorlie
(Goodrich, *Guinevere*, 59).

Although this source indicates that Smervie did not want to
succeed his father as king, his death at the age of twenty-four would
make one wonder whether he did not die before Arthur. Even odder
is that if Smervie had a son in 570, the earliest the child could have
been born, even if Smervie died immediately after conceiving the son
on his wife, is 545, several years after the Battle of Camlann. Or
perhaps this tradition suggests that Arthur lived after the battle, as
some sources have already shown us. We might also wonder why
Smervie died at the young age of twenty-four. Was it while hunting,
and if so, could he have been killed by a boar, making him possibly
the same person as Gwydre?

Norma Goodrich remarks that the *Prose Lancelot* would tend to
confirm that King Arthur had an errant son in Dumbarton

(*Guinevere* 59). It is in the fortress in Dumbarton that Arthur is forced to fall madly in love with Camille through her conjurations, and she then seduces him. Camille was the sister of the Saxon King Hargoda [Hargodabran] states the *Prose Lancelot*; however, the names Camille and Merevie probably encouraged theorists to think Camille and Arthur's foes who imprisoned him were probably Franks, and perhaps they were even members of the Merovingian dynasty. Goodrich suggests that Camille's name was probably more accurately something akin to Krimhild, showing its Saxon background.

As for Merevie or Smervie, Sellar points out that the name is rendered as "Mervin" by Buchanan, "Meirbi" in MS 1467, "Smerbi" in Kilbride, and "Smeirbe" by MacFirbes. He suggests that these may all be variations of "Myrddin" since there seems to be a connection between Smerevie as "the fool of the forest," in the tale of "Eachtra an Amadain Mhoir" or "The Adventures of the Great Fool"—for which see A.J. Bruford's "Gaelic Folk Tales and Medieval Romances" in *Bealoideas* 34 (1966), and the various "Wild Man of the Woods" tales considered by Professor Jackson in "The Motive of the Threefold Death in the story of Suibne Geilt" (Sellar 123). Certainly, traditions exist of Merlin as a wild man in the forest; however, Smervie and Merlin could not be the same person if Smervie were Arthur's son. It is possible, though, if Merlin and Arthur were related, that Myrddin was a family name, or even that Arthur named one of his sons after his great friend and counselor.

That Smerevie could be the son of Arthur is backed up by his being born in An Talla Dearg, the Red Hall. The Galbraiths, who also claim British and not Norman descent, along with the Campbells, are also associated with An Talla Dearg in the Gallic saying: "Britons from the Red Hall, the noblest race in Scotland." "In fact, the name "the Red Hall" occurs in Gaelic folk tales associated with the Arthurian cycle as the name of Arthur's capital: "King Arthur's capital is not Camelot but 'Dunadh an Halla Dheig,' the fortress of the Red Hall, using the English word 'halla.' No English source for the name has been established" (Sellar 120), yet this birthplace could still emphasize not only a British, but a possible Arthurian descent for the Campbells (Sellar 120).

The original Campbell tradition of ancestry is one of British descent. Even the three genealogies that appear to be the least corrupted or manipulated for desirable lineages, still give the Campbells a descent from King Arthur. One always likes to leave open the possibility that some truth lies behind these folktale traditions, but more likely, even these less corrupted genealogies are merely in agreement on what is essentially a myth.

One of the genealogies given traces the descent from Arthur to Smerevie, then continues with a list of clearly fictitious persons of whom nothing interesting is related until the second Fferrither (Sellar 113). From here the genealogy works its way up to Diarmaid and Grainne of the famous Irish love affair (Sellar 115), which we usually assume to be an older story than Arthur's. Obviously, the people who made the genealogy simply stuck in whomever they chose to have for their illustrious ancestors.

However, three more reliable manuscripts exist that do not contain all the fictitious names added to fill up the gap between Arthurian times and the 1200s. These genealogies still give a descent from King Arthur (Sellar 118). Although some of the names in these genealogies differ from one another, there remains the same number of generations from Arthur to his descendant Colin. Sellar suggests that the archaic names in the MacFirbus pedigree may reflect an old particularized descent from a North Briton of the tenth century named Arthur (Sellar 121). Ten generations certainly would not take us from the 1200s when Colin lived, back to the fifth century, and so it may be more reasonable to assume that the Arthur of these genealogies did live in the tenth century; however, the 1467 MS gives Arthur's father's name, and although it is difficult to read, it looks as if it were intended to be Uther (Sellar 117). The Kilbride MS gives Arthur as the son of Ambrosius, and the grandson of Constantine (Sellar 117). Such a coincidence for a father and a grandfather in the tenth century seems more than a coincidence.

The Ten Generations above Colin Mór (Sellar 117)

MS 1467	Kilbride MS	MacFirbis
?IUBUR	AMBROSIUS	IOBHAR
ARTHUR	ARTHUR	ARTHUR
MEIRBI	SMERBI	SMEIRBE
?EIRENAIA	FERADOIG	FERADOIGH
DUIBNE	DUIBNE	DUIBNE
MALCOLM	MALCOLM	MALCOLM
GILLESPIC	DUNCAN	DUNCAN
DUNCAN	GILLESPIC	EOGHAN
DUGALD	DUGALD	DUGALD
GILLESPIC	GILLESPIC	GILLESPIC
COLIN	COLIN	COLIN

It may be very possible then, that the Clan Campbell of Scotland is descended from King Arthur through a forgotten son Smervie. If so, the Clan Campbell is directly descended from King Arthur, leaving the British royal family as merely collateral Arthurian descendants.

The truth will probably never be known, but it seems far more likely that King Arthur, whom we have seen credited with having several children, should have had descendants through at least one of his children, probably a son since a daughter's name is more likely to be forgotten. Furthermore, the tales concerning Mordred and Guinevere's barrenness are just as likely to be fictional as any family's claims to Arthurian descent. As dramatic as the Battle of

Camlann makes the legend, I would prefer to believe that King Arthur lives on in blood as well as in story.

In the following chapter on the minor children in the Middle Ages, while most of these lesser known children mentioned are obviously fictional, we will find another possible Scottish ancestry from the Urquhart family.

Part IV:
The Forgotten and Fictional Children

Chapter 15: The Minor Children in the Middle Ages and Renaissance

Although Mordred has received the greatest attention of Arthur's alleged children in most versions of the Arthurian legends, occasionally writers have also found it desirable to invent new children for Arthur, simply for the sake of adding one more marvelous tale to the Matter of Britain. Although these additional children become far more frequent in modern times, creating such children was also occasionally the case in the Middle Ages.

Medieval writers had a tendency to create new relatives for a hero, but in Arthur's case, Geoffrey of Monmouth's work was almost the definitive source, and he established the tradition in the legend that Arthur could have no children other than Mordred since Guinevere was barren and Constantine, rather than a son of Arthur, succeeded to the throne. Because sons and daughters could not be added, the legends became filled with nephews, the sons of added sisters, to King Arthur, so that each of the heroes in a tale could claim some sort of noble lineage by being the nephew to Arthur (Blaess 77). Many of these nephews would even be familiar storyline characters whom the romancers decided to turn into nephews, and so to explain these many nephews, the successors of these romancers would have to create half-sisters for Arthur (Blaess 74).

Not all romancers tried to be as reasonable, however, and so children were also occasionally created for Arthur; sometimes Guinevere or another woman is the mother of one of these children, while at other times no explanation is given for how they came to be Arthur's children. As a result, as Norris J. Lacy points out, "Arthur may have no children, or only Mordred, or also a legitimate son, or also a daughter" depending on the text (*Arthurian Handbook* xi).

Few medieval Arthurian works credit Arthur with children other than those already discussed, but those few are enough that we should take notice of them.

Probably the earliest minor case of Arthur having a son is in the MSS Harleian 3859 (late tenth century) and Jesus 20 genealogies (fourteenth century) where Arthur has the sons Nougoy and Nennue respectively. In the fictional parts of the *Book of Llandaff* copied 1136-54, Arthur is also credited with a son named Noe or Nouy. The names of the sons are probably enough alike to show that they refer to the same person. However, Tatlock points out that the Arthur here referred to, although believed to be King Arthur because he appears in the Welsh genealogies, is stated to have lived seventeen generations after Constantine the emperor, a period that would probably span about five hundred years; therefore, this Arthur is too late to be the historical Arthur, so this person is really not the son of King Arthur (Tatlock 216-7).

In the Icelandic saga, *Thiðrekssaga*, it states that King Arthur had a daughter named Hilde. The *Thiðrekssaga* tells the adventures of the hero Dietrich von Bern, who is based on the historical Theodoric the Great, the Ostrogoth king who ruled Italy from 493-526 A.D. Several portions of this work include heroes and scenes from the *Nibelungeid*. Both the *Thiðrekssaga* and *Nibelungeid* date to the thirteenth century, although the *Thiðrekssaga* has origins that go back to at least the ninth century.

Neither King Arthur, nor his daughter, have much to do with the saga. Simply as a sidenote in the work, we are told:

> Dietrich, forsaken by Virginal, and anxious to marry again, had, in the mean while, sent his nephew Herbart to Arthur's court in the Bertanga land (Britain), to sue for the hand of Hilde, his fair young daughter. But Arthur, averse to sending his child so far away, would not at first permit the young ambassador to catch a glimpse of her face, and sent her to church guarded by ten warriors, ten monks, and ten duennas.
>
> In spite of all these safeguards, Herbart succeeded in seeing the princess, and after ascertaining that she was very

beautiful, he secured a private interview, and told her of his master's wish to call her wife. Hilde, wishing to know what kind of a man her suitor was, begged Herbart to draw his portrait; but finding him unprepossessing, she encouraged Herbart to declare his own love, and soon eloped with him.

(*Thiðrekssaga*)

Nothing more is said of Herbart or Hilde in the saga. Apparently Dietrich was not overly upset about his nephew stealing his potential bride. Other versions of the story circulated in the Middle Ages as the Herbort and Hildeburg saga, originating in the *Ruoblieb* romance, which travelling minstrels expanded upon. In these stories, Hildeburg is always a princess, usually a Norman one, which still links her then possibly to England, but never again is she named as King Arthur's daughter specifically.

Another early text that credits Arthur with additional children is the *Petit Brut* (1310) by Rauf de Boun. In this work, King Arthur has three sons. The first is named Adeluf III, named for Uther's brother and father, those who are Aurelius Ambrosius and Constantine in Geoffrey of Monmouth, with whom this name seems to have no connection. Arthur's other two sons are Morgan le Noir, whom Arthur loved best, and Patrike the Rous. When King Arthur died, the island of Britain was divided among these three sons. No mention is made of Mordred, and when Arthur dies, after a twenty-one year reign, it is at the castle of Kerlionus, from where his body is carried to Glastonbury.

Rauf de Boun wrote this work for Henry de Lacy, Earl of Lincoln. It is not known whether Rauf wrote it according to the desires of his patron or he simply let his imagination take over. Occasionally he refers to "l'autre Brut" but there is no other known document with anything similar to the stories in his work, so if he had an earlier source, which seems unlikely, it has since been forgotten (Fletcher 210-12).

The next source naming children for King Arthur has an extremely shaky place in Arthurian literature. *Samsoms Saga Fogra* (*Saga of Samson the Fair*) is a fourteenth century Icelandic work linked to the Matter of Britain only because the hero is the son of one King Arthur of England; however, this King Arthur is not the famous Arthur of legend (Lacy, *Arthurian Encylopedia*, 472). Geoffrey of Monmouth does state that King Arthur conquered Iceland in book ix (Geoffrey of Monmouth 222), but this brief remark is the only known connection between King Arthur and Iceland and does not seem to be the source behind *Samsoms Saga Fogra*. In fact, Geoffrey of Monmouth states that after King Arthur's death, Iceland was reconquered by King Malgo in book xi (263).

No more mysterious children of King Arthur appear until Sir Thomas Malory's *Le Morte D'Arthur*. In Book I, Chapter 17 of this work, King Arthur is the father of Borre, whom Loomis believes we can trace back through a hypothetical Gorre to Gwri (*Celtic Myth* 342). However, as we saw in Chapter 3, Lacy believes we can trace Borre back to Llacheu because Borre's mother is said to be Lyoners. She is probably the Lisanor who figures as Llacheu's mother in certain versions (*Arthurian Handbook* 368). Another possibility may be that a lost tradition exists of Lisanor being the mother to more than one of Arthur's sons. If Borre can be traced back to Gwri, whom we have already seen as a possible origin for Gwydre, then could not Lisanor have been Gwydre's mother? Some chroniclers could have been confused and made her Llacheu's mother, when his mother was actually Guinevere. Certainly the name Borre is much closer to Gorre and then Gwydre than it is to any form of Llacheu's name. The name Borre even reminds us of the boar by which Gwydre meets his death.

In the seventeenth century appear a few more obscure references to King Arthur's children which appear to be completely imaginative without any basis in tradition.

Eachtra Mhelóra agus Orlando (*The Adventures of Orlando and Melora*), an Irish story existing in three different sixteenth and seventeenth manuscripts, features Melora as King Arthur's daughter. While it has Celtic, possibly medieval Welsh origins, as suggested by its depictions of Merlin as a type of wild man (Matthews, "Notes," 380), it was also highly influenced by

Ariosto's *Orlando Furioso* (1516-32), probably in the English translation of that work by Sir John Harrington published in 1591. It is the first work to treat Arthur's daughter as a warrior, following similar treatments of the female knight Bradament in *Orlando Furioso* and later Britomart in Spenser's *Faerie Queene* (1590-1596).

In the tale, both Melora and Orlando, son to the King of Thessaly, have dreams which are interpreted as each meaning they will find a great love, and in Orlando's case, the great love will save his life. Orlando then travels to Britain and enters Arthur's court where he meets and falls in love with Melora. Sir Mador becomes jealous and goes to Merlin, requesting that he help him get Orlando out of the way so he will have a chance with Melora. Merlin casts a spell in which Orlando ends up captured and silent in a forest. When Melora learns what has happened, she must embark on a quest for three items that are seemingly impossible to be obtained by a "son of Adam." The three items are the spear of Longinus, a precious stone owned by the King of Narsinga's daughter far in the east, and the oil from the Pig of Tuis which belongs to the King of Asia.

Melora disguises herself as a man, becoming known as the Knight of the Blue Surcoat. Of course, she ultimately obtains all the items required and returns to Britain where she saves Orlando from the spell. King Arthur then agrees to Orlando and Melora's marriage. Sadly, no mention is made of their having children.

Richard Johnson's *Tom a Lincolne* (1607) tells of the adventures of Tom, the natural son of King Arthur and Angellica, the Earl of Lincoln's daughter. The epitome of Tom's good fortune occurs when he marries Prester John's daughter (Lacy, *Arthurian Encyclopedia*, 304). There seems to be no earlier source or tradition behind this work; however, Prester John has other Arthurian appearances. In Wolfram von Eschenbach's *Parzival*, Percival's brother marries Repanse de Schoye, and their son is Prester John. The same story occurs at the end of the *Perlesvaus*. Prester John also makes an appearance in the Italian work *Guerino il Meschino* (1391) by Andrea da Barberino, which was obviously influenced by Arthurian literature. Antonio Viscardi summarizes this work in his chapter "Arthurian Influences on Italian Literature: From 1200 to 1500." The hero of the tale is the son of the King of Apulia and Calabria and his Arab wife, but ignorant of his birth, he is sold as a captive, then proves himself in battle, receives his freedom and becomes a knight errant. He then sets off to find the secret of his birth, which a mysterious voice tells him is one of royalty. Later, he visits the realm of Prester John (Loomis, *Arthurian Literature*, 425-6).

The work which gives Arthur the most abundant number of children all at the same time is the Scottish ballad of *Child Rowland* found in *De Ortu Walwanii*. In this work, King Arthur's daughter, Burd Ellen (Burd is simply a sort of title meaning lady or gentlewoman), is carried away by the fairies to the castle of the King of Elfland. Burd Ellen's three brothers are determined to save her so they go to the warlock Merlin for advice. When consulted, Merlin instructs the eldest brother how to bring his sister back, but the brother fails and is captured by the King of Elfland. The second brother, also with Merlin's advice, attempts to rescue his sister with the same result as that of his older brother. Then the youngest brother, Child Rowland, receives the instruction of Merlin, and travels to Elfland where he finds his sister in a palace. His sister offers him a bowl of bread and milk, but he wisely refuses it. The King of Elfland now bursts into the room, and after a furious fight, Child Rowland subdues him. Child Rowland then forces the King of Elfland to awaken his two elder brothers who are in a trance. The four children of King Arthur then leave the palace in triumph and return to merry Carlisle (*Lanzelet* 223).

Loomis has pointed out that this story has a notable parallel to Ulrich's *Lanzelet* (*Lanzelet* 223). It appears to have been derived from the tale of Blathnat's abduction (Loomis, *Celtic Myth*, 22), and it does seem similar to the capture of Guinevere, although here it is a sister rather than a mother, at least to Llacheu, who needs to be rescued. Otherwise, the source for this story is unknown, and no other sources account for the four children.

Finally is the amazingly thorough genealogy compiled by Sir Thomas Urquhart, *Pantochronachanon* (1652). This work, subtitled

"A peculiar promptuary of time," records the Urquhart family's genealogy in an unbroken line back to Adam and Eve and includes 153 generations. While the work has been ridiculed since its first publication, Urquhart was probably not serious but saw the work as an elaborate joke (Wikipedia). Urquhart, who translated Rabelais into English, hopefully was intelligent enough not to believe this elaborately constructed genealogy, but being a monarchist during the English Civil War, he may have thought it would help promote the monarchy's cause, although it's hard to imagine it would convince anyone of its authenticity. While the modern ancestors from about the eleventh century forward are historical, among the earlier and more questionable ones is Tortolina, the daughter of King Arthur. According to Urquhart:

> NICARCHOS married TORTOLINA.
> On this Tortlina who was the daugh-
>   ter of Arthur of Britain, he begot
> MARSIDALIO.
>
> (Urquhart 166)

The book includes a number system above each entry and above this one it makes clear this event happened in the 4,487th year of the world, that Tortolina is of the 115th generation of the family, and that the child Marsidalio is born in the year 540. If nothing else, 540 A.D. is a very plausible year for Arthur's grandchild to be born. Marsidalio is a boy who goes on to marry Repulita and be the father of Hedomenos. The line continues on until the birth of Sir Thomas Urquhart.

The only scholar to my knowledge ever to make comment upon Tortolina directly is Sir Laurence Gardner in *Bloodline of the Holy Grail*, where he states "Old Registers, such as the *Promptuary of Cromarty*, suggest that Arthur also had a daughter called Tortolina, but she was actually his granddaughter (the daughter of Modred)" (Gardner 151). Gardner does not state what these other "Old Registers" are that refer to Tortolina. Nor does he provide any source for his statement that Tortolina is Arthur's granddaughter or that her father is Mordred. Interestingly, Gardner, who is very interested in genealogy, only notes Mordred and Tortolina among those descendants without any reference to the more likely children to have existed, the Welsh children. While Gardner's books are great fun to read, the lack of sources make them questionable in terms of their reliability. If Tortolina is mentioned in other works, I would be interested to know what they are.

Even with these different stories from the Middle Ages and Renaissance, the number of children created for King Arthur is few. The power of Geoffrey of Monmouth can be attested to since it was nearly two centuries after *The History of the Kings of Britain* that anyone created a son for King Arthur and even the children created since then have become little more than footnotes, having no major influence on the form the legend has taken over the centuries. It is really only within the last one hundred years that the idea of King Arthur having any children other than Mordred has strongly resurfaced as we will see in the following chapter.

Chapter 16: King Arthur's Children in Modern Fiction

King Arthur's children, excluding Mordred, have always played a minor role in the legends, and as we have seen, the popularity of Geoffrey of Monmouth may be responsible for their marginalization in the Middle Ages. However, in a few instances they have appeared in fiction since that time, and in the latter half of the twentieth century they have even made, if not a strong, then a noticeable comeback.

Pre-Twentieth Century Depictions of Arthur's Children

The first work we will consider as modern fiction here is Henry Fielding's play *The Tragedy of Tragedies, or the Life and Death of Tom Thumb the Great* (1731). This play's connection to the Arthurian legends is extremely distant, only containing the traditional King Arthur and Merlin. King Arthur's wife is here named Dollallolla, and the daughter of the couple is Huncamunca. The plot includes Tom Thumb, of dwarf stature, famed for slaying giants, who must compete for Huncamunca's hand with Lord Grizzle. After the two suitors fight, Tom Thumb wins and proceeds then to the castle to marry Huncamunca, but on the way he is swallowed by a cow, thereby meeting his end just as Merlin prophesied his death. When the messenger brings the sad news to the court, the queen, who also loved Tom Thumb, repays the messenger for his sad news by slaying him. The messenger's wife then slays the queen in revenge. Huncamunca then slays her mother's murderer, and a courtier named Doodle slays Huncamunca for an old grudge. In the end, everyone but King Arthur has been killed, and then he kills himself, thereby ending the foolish story.

Throughout the play, Huncamunca is unable to make up her mind whom to marry, and then decides she is willing to take two husbands; however, both she and her would-be husbands die before any marriage can take place, which means she has no children and therefore, King Arthur's line dies out. Although Fielding was not trying to write serious Arthurian literature, but rather, he was satirizing the stage plays of his time, I for one am thankful that Fielding did not create any more ridiculous children for King Arthur.

The next work to give King Arthur a child, again a daughter, is far better in plot though no more flattering of Arthur's child. This work is "The Druid's Tale," an interpolation in Sir Walter Scott's "The Bridal of Triermain" (1813). The Druid claims "The mystic tale by bard and sage/Is handed down from Merlin's age" (canto I, ix). The tale states that one day while King Arthur was journeying, he came to a castle in a vale, and inside the castle were one hundred damsels who played at undressing him, and Arthur yielded to them. The queen of the damsels was Guendolen, with whom Arthur dallied for the three months of summer in her garden of delight. Arthur swore to Guendolen that if she bore him a son, he would inherit the kingdom, and if it were a daughter, he would find her a suitable husband. Arthur then leaves Guendolen's castle and when he looks back the castle has disappeared.

Fifteen years later, Arthur is holding court when into his presence comes a huntress, whom he first thinks is Guendolen, but then he realizes it is his own daughter, the huntress, Gyneth. Arthur gives to her Strathclyde, Reged and Carlisle's fortress and town as her dowry. A tournament is then held in which Gyneth becomes champion. When Arthur bids her stop the fight before all his warriors have died, she refuses to obey him. Merlin then appears and punishes Gyneth by condemning her to sleep alone in her vale until she is awakened. Eventually, all adventurers cease searching for her, and so she sleeps until the trumpet of doom which is where the Druid ends his tale.

The only Arthurian work during the Victorian period that concerns us is Dora Stuart Menteath's *Avalon: A Poetic Romance,* published in 1894. This work does not contain a child of King Arthur, but rather a descendant of Mordred who lives in the Victorian Age. This descendant achieves the elixir of life but dies before he can drink it.

Strangely enough, the first work to grant Arthur children in the twentieth century is not a novel, but Rutland Boughton's choral dramas or oratorios called *King Arthur Had Three Sons* which appeared around 1905 (Lacy, *Arthurian Handbook*, 274). The work is of no importance to the legend but rather nonsensical. The lyrics are based on an old English folk song, and are as follows:

> King Arthur had three sons
> That he had
> He had three sons of yore,
> And he kicked 'em out of the door
> Because they could not sing
> Because they could not sing
> Because they could not sing
> That he did
> He had three sons of yore,
> And he kicked 'em out o' door
> Because they could not sing
> The first he was a miller
> That he was, that he was,
> The second he was a weaver
> That he was, that he was,
> And the third, he was a little tailor boy,
> And he was mighty clever
> And he was mighty clever
> And he was mighty clever
> That he was
> And he was mighty clever
> And he was mighty clever
> And he was mighty clever,
> That he was
> The miller stole some grist for his mill
> And the weaver stole some loom

And the little tailor boy
He stole some corduroy
To keep those three rogues warm
To keep those three rogues warm
That he did
And the little tailor boy
He stole some corduroy
To keep those three rogues warm.
Oh the miller he was drowned in his dam
And the weaver he was killed at his loom
And old Nick he cut his stick with the little tailor boy
With the broad-cloth under his arm
With the broad-cloth under his arm
That he did
With the broad-cloth under his arm
And old Nick he cut his stick with the little tailor boy
With the broad-cloth under his arm
That he did. (Boughton 38-48)

Twentieth and Twenty-First Century Depictions of King Arthur's Children

In the last half-century, as numerous Arthurian novels have flooded the market, a growing trend has arisen to create new children for King Arthur. Beginning with Rosemary Sutcliff's *Sword at Sunset* (1963) and continuing into more recent novels such as those by Patricia Kennealy-Morrison and Bernard Cornwell, new children have continually been created, and their roles have become increasingly more significant. Even films like Disney's *A Kid in King Arthur's Court* (1995) and the television film *Guinevere* (1994) have created new children for King Arthur. This creation of children other than Mordred reflects a new direction in Arthurian fiction which may ultimately alter the legend's traditionally tragic ending. This change results from a renewed interest in the Arthurian legend, originally connected with archeological excavations designed to find the historical King Arthur, or at least a better understanding of the

"Arthurian" period. This interest in the historical King Arthur has resulted in novelists trying to place their stories in a more historical and realistic Arthurian world. Despite these historical efforts, most novelists have not gone back to the earlier Welsh traditions as their sources for Arthur's children, Bernard Cornwell being an exception. The earliest attempts to create children in modern fiction were minor, and as in the medieval works, the children were either illegitimate and unimportant, or they died before Arthur's own death. Other novelists have created significant roles for Arthur's children, some of whom even outlive Arthur. Such creations reflect an effort to stretch the legend beyond its tragic conclusion.

Part of the Arthurian tradition's tragedy is that Arthur and Guinevere can produce no child to succeed him, so the throne will eventually be inherited by Mordred, Arthur's bastard son, born of incest. When Arthur and Mordred both die at Camlann, Arthur's bloodline ends, and the throne passes to his distant relative, Constantine. With the creation of new children for Arthur, novelists are working against the neat closure demanded by medieval texts; instead, such novels open up the possibility that Arthur's death need not be so grim, for if he has children, other than Mordred, he and his ideals will live on in his successor to Britain's throne.

That several novelists have been bold enough to create new and significant children for Arthur, thus threatening the traditional tragic ending of the legend, may reflect a modern day desire to feel a connection to the Arthurian world. As I noted at the beginning of this book, an interest in genealogy provides a new sense of connection to the past. Furthermore, the desire for a connection to the Arthurian world surfaced as recently as during the tragic death of Diana, Princess of Wales in 1997. The princess' burial upon an island in the middle of a lake was immediately connected with Arthur's passing to Avalon. Furthermore, several people hope that when Diana's son, Prince William, becomes king, he will adopt his second name, making him King Arthur.

In the last few decades, novelists have tried to build upon this psychological desire to provide some sort of link between the Arthurian world and the present day. Originally, novelists who attempted to create new children for Arthur realized it would mean the tragic ending of the story would have to be altered. Rather than risk changing the legend's conclusion, these new children were made to die before Arthur. As creating new children for Arthur became more frequent, however, more novelists also attempted to stretch the legend, making these children more significant, thereby, making Arthur's death somewhat less tragic. The modern novels that create children for Arthur can be separated into two categories—those which are predominantly traditional, placing Arthur's children only in minor roles, and those novels which seek to project Arthur's bloodlines beyond his own lifetime, thus altering or transforming the traditionally tragic ending of the legend.

Children with Minor Roles

The first modern novel to create a new child for King Arthur was Rosemary Sutcliff's *Sword at Sunset* (1963). In this novel, Artos has a daughter by his wife, Guenhamara. Guenhamara begins labor while she is with Artos during a war campaign, so Artos finds shelter for her among the Dark People in their fairy hills. After a daughter, Hylin, is born, Guenhamara remains too weak to travel, so Artos leaves her at the fairy dwelling for three days while he continues his work. The same night Guenhamara had given birth to her daughter, one of the fairy women bore a sickly child. When Hylin dies shortly after her first birthday, Guenhamara blames Artos for leaving them in the fairy dwelling because she believes the Dark People drained the strength from her daughter to save the fairy woman's child. Artos and Guenhamara have no other children, so Sutcliff's novel continues along the legend's traditional lines, leaving Artos without any direct descendants to succeed him. The possibility that Arthur could have a daughter, however, interested Sutcliff's sucessors, who would adopt and elaborate upon the idea.

The next appearance of a daughter for Arthur was in Barbara Ferry Johnson's *Lionors* (1975). Johnson goes back to Malory, loosely basing her novel on Malory's story of how Arthur has a son, Borre, whose mother is Lionors, the daughter of an earl named Sanam. All Malory further tells us of Borre is that he became a

Knight of the Round Table (Malory 42). Johnson transforms Malory's story, having Arthur beget upon Lionors a blind bastard girl named Elise. Johnson, like Sutcliff, is toying with the idea that Arthur could have had a child, yet Johnson also removes any possibility that this child could succeed Arthur. Like Sutcliff's Hylin, this child is a girl, the wrong sex for a claimant to the throne. Even if a woman could rule the kingdom, it is inconceivable that anyone would follow a blind queen. Finally, when Elise grows up, she decides to enter a convent rather than to marry or have children, thus preventing the possibility of Arthur having future descendants. Johnson's blind girl presents no threat to the traditional ending of the legend because when Arthur dies, he has no heir to succeed him.

Catherine Christian's novel *The Sword and the Flame: Variations on a Theme of Sir Thomas Malory* (published in the United States as *The Pendragon*) (1979) also simply toys with the idea that Arthur might have children. Here Guinevere is barren, so Arthur has some unnamed mistresses by whom he produces illegitimate children. These children never appear in the novel but are merely passing references in conversation. In one scene, Bedivere discusses with Mawgan, the Morgan le Fay of this novel, whether it is Guinevere or Arthur who is responsible for there being no heir to the throne. Mawgan remarks, "Arthur's a proven sire to common knowledge. Does not Lein, who carries his standard now, favor him beyond disputing—and I've heard of others. Most men blame the queen" (Christian 308). Later, when discussing the succession with Arthur, Bedivere remarks, "You've sired good stock in your time, Bear. No need to read a slur where none's intended. I doubt any Companion of the Council, or any man in the host, for that matter, lays the blame of failure at your door" (412). Here, Arthur even has sons, but illegitimacy bars his descendants from inheriting the throne.

Another novel where Arthur's descendants are merely mentioned and never seen is Parke Godwin's *Firelord* (1980). Here, Arthur begets Mordred on the Pict woman, Morgana. Many years later, Arthur is married to Guinevere, but he still feels fondness for Morgana. When Mordred is an adult, Arthur offers to let Morgana and Mordred and their families come live with him at Camelot.

Upon his arrival, Mordred informs Arthur that he has his own son and daughter, but rather than bring them with him, he left them outside the castle walls because he does not trust Guinevere. When Arthur is off his guard, Guinevere orders Morgana killed while Mordred escapes. After Arthur and Mordred fall at Camlann, no further mention is made of Mordred's children. However, they are unimportant to the succession anyway, for a Pict would not have been accepted as Arthur's successor.

Nancy McKenzie's *The High Queen* (1995) also refers to Mordred as having children. These children, however, are never named, and they are born to various different women with whom Mordred has relations. Because they are the bastards of a son who becomes Arthur's enemy, it is unlikely that these grandchildren of Arthur will succeed him.

Another novel to give Arthur a descendant with a minor role is Anne Eliot Crompton's *Merlin's Harp* (1997). The novel's main character is Niviene, daughter of the Lady of the Lake, who lives with her mother in Avalon. One day, Arthur, while hunting a deer, enters into Avalon and meets Niviene, who seduces him. Niviene is unaware that the hunter is King Arthur; nor will she realize her lover's identity until twenty years later when she travels with Merlin to Arthur's court. Niviene gives birth to a son named Bran, who is very self-sufficient; at age five, he sets up his own hidden house in the forest. When Niviene has not seen her son for several days, she becomes worried because she senses a type of energy in the forest which she fears has pulled her son away.

Unknown to Niviene, Merlin has taken Bran away to be raised by Morgan le Fey. Morgan has changed Bran's name to Mordred, and she teaches him to hate Arthur. When Mordred reaches adulthood, he begins to plot with Morgan le Fey against his father. He also falls in love with a girl named Aefa, who becomes pregnant with his child. Before the child is born, Mordred and Arthur fight and die at Camlann. As Niviene is holding the dying Mordred in her arms, she reads his memory and realizes he is her long lost son, Bran. After Mordred's death, Aefa gives birth to Mordred's daughter, Dana. Niviene and Aefa take the newborn child to live with them at Avalon, thus removing her from the court and any chance of inheriting Arthur's throne.

In contrast to these novels, the made for television film *Guinevere* (1994) creates a child whom the film at least claims will be significant. This film also claims to be based on Persia Woolley's Guinevere novels, but in reality, not the slightest noticeable connection exists between the film and the novels. In the novels, Guinevere never gives birth to a child because after she is raped by Maelgwn, she is unable to bear children.

In the film, Guinevere does become pregnant by Arthur. During Guinevere's pregnancy, however, Morgan le Fay attempts to poison Guinevere and kill Arthur's child. Desperate to protect her unborn baby, Guinevere flees to a peasant's hut where she gives birth to a daughter. To save the child from Morgan le Fay, Guinevere allows everyone to think the child died at birth while she actually leaves her daughter to be raised by a peasant woman. Not even Arthur realizes his daughter is still alive, and believing Guinevere is now barren after her supposed miscarriage, he seeks to comfort her by saying, "This island will be our children."

Later in the film, Arthur is captured by Maelgwn, who is in league with Morgan to take over Britain. While Arthur is a prisoner, Merlin comes to Guinevere and tells her that her child is safe on the Isle of Anglesey. Then Merlin prophesies of the child, "One day she will return like her father to save her country"; for the present, however, it is Guinevere who must save Britain by rescuing Arthur. Once Arthur is saved, and Morgan and Maelgwn's plans are foiled, the film ends, never further hinting at the future of Arthur and Guinevere's daughter; however, Merlin's prophecy that Arthur's daughter will return to save her country recalls the statement made in Ulrich von Zatzikhoven's *Lanzelet* that Llacheu (here called Loüt) went "with Arthur, his noble father, into a country whence the Bretons still expect both of them evermore" (119), but this similarity is probably only coincidental.

All of the above treatments of Arthur's children merely play with the possibility that Arthur could have children other than Mordred, or even descendants who outlive Mordred and him. Eventually, each work shies away from making these children prominent enough to upset the status quo of the kingdom or the legend's tragic ending. While Arthur may have children, the children are deprived from inheriting Arthur's throne for any one of numerous reasons including dying young, being female, being blind, being illegitimate, being of the wrong race, being descended from the traitor Mordred, or in the case of *Guinevere*, ending the story before Arthur dies, and thus never fulfilling the promise made about the child. While each of these works is interesting in its treatment of Arthur's children, each treatment is minor and easily forgettable. In contrast, other writers have stretched the legend farther by allowing newly created children or descendants of King Arthur to play more prominent roles.

Children with Major Roles

The first novel to treat seriously the creation of a child for Arthur is the last in a trilogy by Vera Chapman, entitled *King Arthur's Daughter* (1976). Arthur's daughter is named Ursulet, a name Chapman tells us in the foreword, she derived from the constellation Ursa Minor since King Arthur is often associated with the constellation, Ursa Major, meaning the great bear. Chapman adds, "Nobody can say that King Arthur did *not* have a daughter. Kings' daughters, unless they make dynastic marriages, are apt to slip out of history and be ignored" (Chapman 7); Ursulet, therefore, is Arthur's daughter, whom history forgot to record.

The novel begins when Ursulet is an infant, while Arthur's other child, Mordred, is already an adult. Arthur has placed in writing that Ursulet will inherit his throne, while Mordred, because of his tendency toward evil, will be made an earl and owe allegiance to Ursulet. When Ursulet is still a child, attending a convent school, Arthur dies in battle against the Saxons. The Saxons attack the convent where Ursulet lives, causing her to flee and escape into the forest. After wandering about, Ursulet is taken in by a family of Jutes who make her their servant girl, and as the years pass, she begins to forget her royal heritage.

Meanwhile, a young boy named Ambris is taken by his great-aunt, Lynett, to Sir Bedivere to become a knight. Bedivere is also the knight who holds the piece of parchment in which Arthur declared that Ursulet would be his heir. Ambris is now instructed by Bedivere and Lynett to go on quest to find Ursulet so the rightful ruler of Britain may sit on the throne.

After several adventures, Ambris finds Ursulet and convinces her to come with him; Ursulet now begins to remember her royal heritage. Before she can claim the throne, however, Ursulet, along with Ambris, is chased by freakish creatures toward Mordred's castle. Mordred introduces Ursulet to his two sons, Morcar, who at sixteen is already said to have fathered a dozen bastards, and Morwen, age fifteen, who is usually frightened and is considered useless by his father. Mordred locks up Ambris, while trying to force Ursulet into marrying Morcar, but with the help of Lynett, Ursulet and Ambris escape, taking Morwen, who has become their ally, with them through the caves under Mordred's castle.

When Mordred discovers the escape of Ursulet and her companions, he has his men await them at the place where the underground caverns end. Lynett, however, leads Ursulet's party through the caverns toward another exit she remembers from years ago. Along this passage, they arrive at the chamber where King Arthur sleeps until the hour when Britain will need him. Arthur now awakes, thinking it is time for his return. He soon realizes his mistake, but before going back to sleep, he marries Ambris and Ursulet: "Ursulet, Ambrosius, I join you," he said. "Remember what I have done. For you must carry on the line of those who look for my returning" (95). Arthur then describes the creation of this line:

> "Mark this. Men give their names to their sons, and the mother's name is forgotten. And if the line from father to son is broken, the name is lost. But the mother-line—ah, that runs on, hidden and forgotten, but always there. You my child—to be the mother of those that believe in me. Thousands of them—millions of them—mother to daughter, without name or record. No kings—but Queens a few, and commoners without number—here a soldier, there a poet, there a traveller in strange places, a priest, a

sage—from their mothers they take it—some pass it to their daughters—"

"What father?" she whispered bending her face to his. "What do they take and pass?"

"The fire," he answered. "The fire that is Britain. The spark in the flint, the light in the crystal, the sword in the stone. Yours, and your children's." (95)

Morwen then asks his grandfather, Arthur, whether he has any words for him. Arthur replies, "Morwen...Ah, pity, pity. I could have made a man of you. I could have made a knight of you. At least do not slay your brother" (95-6).

Arthur then tells Ursulet, "My crown is yours, but you will not rule in Britain. Not now. Not yet" (96). Before returning to sleep, Arthur's final words are, "I shall come again. Let Britain remember—I shall come again" (96).

Ursulet's party now makes its way out of the cave, whose exit takes them to Glastonbury Tor on the morning of May 1st, where all Ursulet's loyal people have come to see her crowned both Queen of May and Queen of Britain.

In anger at Ursulet's escape and crowning, Mordred sends his army to attack Ursulet's troops. In the battle, Morcar kills his younger brother, Morwen, and then Lynett kills Morcar, while Ambris kills Mordred. But before Ursulet's army can claim the victory, the Saxons attack and defeat them. Ursulet becomes unconscious during the battle, only to awake a week later in Gwent. Lynett then tells her that the Saxons are now masters of the kingdom, so it would be hopeless to try defeating them. Ambris and Ursulet feel all they tried to do was in vain, but Lynett, remembering the words Arthur had told them, says:

> No, not in vain. Like a plant that dies down in the winter, and guards its seed to grow again, so you two must raise the lineage from which all Arthur's true followers are to grow—not by a royal dynasty, but by spreading unknown and unnoticed, along the distaff line—mother to daughter, father to daughter, mother to son. Names and

titles shall be lost, but the story and the spirit of Arthur shall not be lost. For Arthur is a land and Arthur is the land of Britain. And the time shall come when the Saxons, yes the Saxons shall pay homage to Arthur too—yes, and other races we do not know yet...But in the end, Cymry and Saxon, and others from over the sea, will all be one, and all will know the name of Arthur. And there will be those among them, like a thread in a tapestry, who are your descendants, many, many generations to come. Here, in your safe retreat in the mountains of Gwent, you shall be Arthur's Adam and Eve. So shall Arthur conquer, not by one war, nor by one kingship, that soon passes away, but by the carriers of the spirit that does not die. Not by any son of Arthur, born to take the sword and perish by the sword—but by the daughter of Arthur, born to give life to those that come after. (143-4)

King Arthur's Daughter definitely changes the legend by creating a novel that primarily takes place after Arthur's death and provides for the passing of the throne to one of his heirs. It is the only work since Geoffrey of Monmouth's *Historia Regum Britanniae* to provide Mordred with two sons, although these sons kill each other rather than being killed by Constantine, as Geoffrey states (262). While the novel does not allow Arthur's child to inherit the throne, the novel is important for being the first modern work to suggest that Arthur's descendants live beyond the sixth century, suggesting possible genealogical and spiritual links between the Arthurian and the modern periods. *King Arthur's Daughter* has not received a great deal of critical attention, but it is significant in leaving a glimpse of hope, not just in a story or a dream, but in actual descendants of Arthur who will carry his bloodline into the future.

Surprisingly, the same year that *King Arthur's Daughter* appeared, *The Grey King* (1976), the fourth book in Susan Cooper's *The Dark Is Rising* series, was also published. This series attempts a more direct connection between the Arthurian period and modern times by allowing the Arthurian characters to time travel into the twentieth century. In *The Grey King* we learn that Arthur and

Guinevere had a son named Bran. Because Guinevere had been untrue to her husband before, she feared Arthur would kill the child, not believing it was his own. Therefore, Guinevere came out of the past into the twentieth century through the enchantment of a magical creature called the dewin so that the child could grow up safely in the future with a Welsh family. During the twentieth century, Bran grows into a young boy who helps in the fight against the powers of the Dark, while thinking he is a twentieth century Welsh boy. At the end of the novel, Bran learns he is really Arthur and Guinevere's son.

Bran's story continues into the fifth and final book of the series, *Silver on the Tree* (1977). In this novel, King Arthur appears in the twentieth century to defeat the powers of the Dark. Arthur states that this moment is his second coming, so no one need wait for him to come again. Saving the universe from the Dark is a greater deed than any Arthur is credited with in the legends, yet to know that Arthur has had his second coming and will not come again is a disappointment to a lover of Arthurian lore, for the reader may wish personally to have experienced Arthur's return.

Before Arthur leaves the twentieth century, he asks his son to go with him "to the land of apples trees," but Bran decides that after living so many years in the twentieth century, he belongs to it and will remain there. Arthur explains that Bran will now no longer be the son of the Pendragon, but rather Bran Davies, the son of his Welsh foster-father. The novel concludes with Arthur's departure, while Bran is left to live a normal life in twentieth century Wales.

In 1991 appeared Mary J. Jones' *Avalon*. This novel provides some difficulty because doubt exists about whether the main character, Argante, is really Arthur's daughter. Furthermore, Argante is a lesbian, leaving no hope that Arthur's line will continue or his descendants succeed him. The novel begins with Lancelot bringing a baby girl to Avalon to protect it from Arthur. This baby girl is named Gwyr, but the people of Avalon decide she will be named Argante. Argante is the daughter of Gwenhyfar, but Gwenhyfar is not sure whether the child's father is Lancelot or Arthur. Argante, as the novel's narrator, explains her parentage as:

My mother was Gwenhyfar, my father Lancelot or Arthur. I do not know which. Neither did my mother. She leaned toward Lancelot, but only, I think, because she loved him more. I resemble her: the same plain, square face, the same fair hair and high thin nose, but I have grey eyes, like Arthur. On the other hand, I am tall, much taller than my mother, taller even than Arthur. And Lancelot is very tall. In the end, I suppose it doesn't matter whose child I am. Neither wished to claim me—Lancelot because he wanted to spare my life (so my mother said) and Arthur because he thought me Lancelot's child. (10-11)

Throughout her childhood, Argante hopes Arthur will acknowledge her as his daughter, but he never does. In fact, Argante only sees Arthur once in the novel, and the only other major Arthurian character who makes an important appearance is Medraut, who is also Arthur's child here. The novel's plot centers around an attempt by Annis, Queen of the Wastelands, to conquer Britain, in which she enlists Medraut's help. The novel appears to be heavily influenced by Marion Zimmer Bradley's *Mists of Avalon* (1982), for most of the attention is given to Avalon and its matriarchal system. Consequently, the women rely upon one another, rather than men, resulting in many lesbian relationships. The climax occurs when Medraut kidnaps Argante's female lover, Elin, and Argante must rescue her. After Elin is rescued, she and Argante celebrate their soul-friend ceremony (235). The main plot centers upon the development of Elin and Argante's love relationship, leaving the villains, Medraut and Annis, still threatening Britain at the novel's end. Because what little of a plot exists in the novel concerns marginal or new Arthurian characters, it adds little to a new interpretation or understanding of the Arthurian legend, intending rather to give a feminist lesbian loose reading to the story. Since Argante is a lesbian, the novel leaves no hope that she will ever bear children, so while the lesbian theme attempts to make a connection between twentieth century issues and the Arthurian world, the connection is not promoted by the possibility of genealogical connections as do most of the other novels which give major treatments of Arthur's children.

Elizabeth C. Wein's *The Winter Prince* (1993) creates two new children for Arthur, who serve as a means to create a new interpretation of Mordred, here called Medraut. Medraut is the child of incest, created by the coupling of Artos and his evil sister, Morgause. However, Artos later married Ginevra, and by her he has produced two children, the twins Goewin, a daughter, and her younger brother, Lleu. Although Lleu is the youngest of Artos' three children, he is the only legitimate male child, and therefore, he is to inherit Artos' throne. From the time that these twins are born, Medraut feels hatred toward them, knowing they have ruined his hope of someday becoming king. Artos knows, however, that because Lleu is a sickly boy, he will only be king in name, while Medraut's intelligence will be needed to run the kingdom, so Artos determines that Medraut will serve as Lleu's regent. Medraut is torn between his loyalty to father and younger brother and the control his mother holds over him, for Morgause seeks to destroy Artos and place Medraut on the throne. Lleu slowly comes to despise Medraut for being conceived in incest and controlled by Morgause. When Lleu declares to Medraut that he finds him disgusting, Medraut becomes angry and decides he will help his mother destroy Lleu (144). Medraut, under the pretense of taking his brother and sister hunting, now kidnaps Lleu and Goewin with the help of one of his mother's other sons, Agrivain. Medraut believes Artos loves Lleu enough to sacrifice the throne for his younger son, so Medraut releases Goewin to return to Artos' castle of Camlan and tell Artos that Lleu will be killed unless Artos names Medraut as his heir. Lleu, however, gains command of the situation and demands that Medraut and Agrivain bring him back to Camlan. When they are near Camlan, Agrivain is allowed to depart while Medraut and Lleu return home. Often during this time together, the half-brothers have struggled for power over each other; at times, Medraut has been tempted to kill Lleu, but Medraut's real struggle is overcoming the psychological power that his mother, Morgause, holds over him. Because Lleu has always been sickly, he weakens toward the journey's end and can no longer travel. Finally, Medraut refuses to be controlled by his mother any longer. In a moving scene, he carries his brother back to Camlan. Lleu admits he has always admired his older brother, while Medraut realizes and confesses that he loves Lleu. When they reach Camlan, Artos is pleased to see the brothers reconciled, and he remarks that now Medraut has finally changed Lleu so that he will be strong enough to serve as king. Medraut replies that Lleu changed both of them. Now Medraut will always loyally serve his younger brother. This reconciliation concludes the interesting psychological exploration of Medraut. The novel closes with the understanding that Lleu will become king after Artos, again defying the medieval tradition that Arthur dies without heirs.

A decade later, Wein published the first of four novels that are sequels to *The Winter Prince* which because they were published so much later are not quite a natural progression from this work, so I will discuss them below where they chronologically belong.

Another work seeking to connect the Arthurian world to the twentieth century in a much different way is the Disney film *A Kid in King Arthur's Court* (1995), based on the famous Mark Twain novel. Here King Arthur has two daughters, Sarah, and her younger sister Katherine, or Katey. Guinevere, the girls' mother, is deceased. The hero of the film is Calvin Fuller, a twentieth-century fourteen-year old baseball player from California whom Merlin accidentally brings to Britain while searching for a hero who can save Camelot from the evil Lord Belasco. King Arthur has become old and ineffectual since the death of his wife, so he is unaware of Lord Belasco's crimes against the people. Belasco wishes to seize all power by marrying Arthur's older daughter, Sarah. Sarah, however, has refused to marry because she is in love with a young trainer of knights, Kane, who because of his low social status, is unsuitable for a princess to marry. Arthur has decided Sarah must marry someone, and since she will not choose a husband, a tournament is to be held, the champion of which will win the princess' hand and become heir to the throne. Meanwhile, the only hope the poor people have from the evil of Lord Belasco is the kindness of the Black Knight, a mysterious Robin Hood figure, whom Arthur mistakenly believes is a villain.

Lord Belasco, being too cowardly to joust in the tournament and win Princess Sarah's hand, attempts to coerce her into marriage by kidnapping her sister, Katey. Calvin realizes what is happening, however, so he informs King Arthur, and together they rescue Katey. Lord Belasco now fights in the tournament, defeating his opponents until only he and Kane are left to do battle with each other. Through misfortune, Belasco defeats Kane and is about to claim Sarah's hand when the Black Knight suddenly appears and defeats Belasco. Arthur now asks the Black Knight to reveal his identity, and all are amazed when the Black Knight removes his helmet to display that he is really the Princess Sarah. Arthur says Sarah has now earned the right to choose whom she will marry, so of course, she chooses Kane. Sarah and Kane are named as heirs to the kingdom while Belasco is forever banished.

While the emphasis in the film is largely upon Calvin's budding romance with Katey and the twentieth century items that Calvin introduces to Camelot, the end of the story is remarkable because it allows a daughter of Arthur to be the real hero. There is no Mordred here, and even Lord Belasco is never a convincing threat, so the throne will safely pass to Arthur's descendants by his daughter, Sarah. The film leaves every hint that Arthur's kingdom will remain stable and instead of a tragic ending, a peaceful succession will occur upon King Arthur's death. The film ends with Calvin being knighted and then returned home with the help of Merlin's magic. The last scene shows Calvin hitting a home run during a baseball game. Arthur and Katey suddenly appear in the twentieth century to help celebrate this success.

Perhaps the work that takes the most liberty with the Arthurian legend, and therefore, opens itself to create larger roles for Arthur's children and descendants is *The Keltiad* series by Patricia Kennealy-Morrison. The author intended to write eighteen novels in the series, but after publication of the eighth novel, the publisher HarperCollins decided to drop the series. The Arthurian world of these novels is placed in outer space, allowing the stories a freedom beyond a typical medieval setting in Britain. The premise behind the series is that a group of Keltic people left earth in 453 C.E. in their spaceships and travelled to outer space to create a new kingdom, Keltia.

Only three novels in *The Keltiad* series deal specifically with Arthur and are known as the "Tales of Arthur"; they include *The Hawk's Gray Feather* (1990), *The Oak Above the Kings* (1994) and *The Hedge of Mist* (1996). The plot of this trilogy is long and complicated, but the length provides for an extensive treatment of Arthur's descendants and their history.

At the opening of the "Tales of Arthur" trilogy, some fifteen centuries have passed since the Kelts first left earth in the fifth century. The nation of Keltia is now divided between the royal House of Don, which is in exile, and the evil Archdruid Edeyrn who has usurped the kingdom. The plot of the first two novels is how Arthur, heir to the House of Don, regains the kingdom.

Arthur has four children over the course of this trilogy, although none of these children is Mordred. There is a character, Mordryth, who is Arthur's nephew, the son of his evil half-sister Marguessan, but although Mordryth is a villain, Arthur outlives his nephew. Arthur's own death is in a sort of black hole where his spaceship becomes trapped. Even though he disappears from Keltia when he enters this black hole, Arthur promises his people he will return. The Kelts decide the throne will pass to Arthur's heirs, but the ruler will always hold the kingdom as a type of regent until Arthur's return whenever that may be.

The first child born to Arthur is Malgan in *The Hawk's Gray Feather*. During the wars with Edeyrn, Arthur takes a mistress named Gwenwynbar, who follows him about on his campaigns. However, Arthur's men do not like Gwenwynbar, and because Arthur will not make her his queen, she decides to leave him and join his enemies' side. Soon after, Gwenwynbar becomes the wife of Owain, who is Edeyrn's heir. Seven months after this marriage, Gwenwynbar gives birth to a son, Malgan. Throughout the remainder of the trilogy, the question remains whether Malgan is Arthur or Owain's son. Unfortunately, the genealogy charts at the end of the book give away the suspense by showing he is Arthur's child. After Arthur defeats Edeyrn and Owain, Gwenwynbar plots against Arthur, but her plots are discovered and she is put to death. Arthur adopts and raises Malgan, wanting to believe the boy is his own. Malgan, however, grows up holding a grudge against Arthur for the death of his mother. Malgan soon joins his evil aunt Marguessan in her plans to take over the kingdom. Arthur tries to reconcile with Malgan, but eventually, they battle and Malgan is slain while Arthur survives.

In *The Oak Above the Kings*, Arthur marries his cousin, Gweniver, but their marriage remains without issue for many years. Now that Edeyrn is defeated, Arthur seeks to punish those foreign nations which allied themselves to Edeyrn. During this campaign, Arthur visits the planet Aojun and has an affair with the princess, Majanah. Their relationship produces a daughter, Donah, who divides her time between the worlds of Aojun and Keltia. When Marguessan steals the Grail, Donah adopts the role traditionally held by Percival's sister in Arthurian legend of the female who assists in finding the Grail. Donah also assumes Guinevere's traditional role of being kidnapped by Melwas. When Donah reaches adulthood, she marries a man named Harodin, and we are told she has "three children, including her heir, Sarinah" (*Hedge* 449). After Donah's mother, Majanah, dies, Donah becomes the next queen of the planet Aojun.

After many years of barrenness, Gweniver also produces children for Arthur, first a son, Arawn, who after Arthur's death, becomes king and is thought "a worthy successor to his great parents" (*Hedge* 432). Gweniver also gives birth to a daughter, Arwenna, who is not born until after Arthur's death. While the novels do not say much about these children's futures, the genealogy charts indicate that Arawn has a child, Arianwen, who rules Keltia after him, and Arianwen also has children. Arthur's daughter, Arwenna, has a child named Blythan, who also produces children. Finally, the charts indicate that Donah's heir, Sarinah, also has descendants not pictured on the chart.

Kennealy-Morrison's novels, therefore, create an extensive family tree that continues beyond King Arthur, providing for his descendants to succeed him as rulers of the kingdom. Toward the end of *The Hedge of Mist*, Taliesin, Arthur's brother-in-law and the novels' narrator, has a vision of the future, in which he sees a great queen who will look like Arthur and Gweniver from whom she will be descended (287). Though not named, this queen is doubtless Aeron, the heroine of another of the Keltiad trilogies, the "Tales of Aeron," which were written before the "Tales of Arthur" but chronologically follow the "Tales of Arthur." The novels in the "Tales of Aeron" also contain more genealogy charts which detail Aeron's descent from Arthur and Gweniver for over nine generations. Because these novels do not deal with Arthur or his children specifically, they will not be discussed further, but they do continue Kennealy-Morrison's vision of an Arthurian family tree that extends centuries after Arthur's passing.

By setting her novels in outer space, Kennealy-Morrison does not provide Arthur with a bloodline that connects him to the humans of twentieth century earth. Rather the "Tales of Arthur" novels take place in the twenty-first century, while the "Tales of Aeron" are set in the thirty-fifth and thirty-sixth centuries. However, this outer space setting is also what leaves the novels open for such extensive creation of descendants for Arthur, providing interesting possibilities for the legend, even if they are greatly removed from the traditional story.

Another series with just a fairly loose connection to Arthur's children is Stephen King's *The Dark Tower* series. The main character of these novels is a gunslinger, Roland of Gilead. In the fourth of the seven novels in the series, *Wizard and Glass* (1997), we learn Roland is the son of:

> Steven Deschain of Gilead, a gunslinger (which was to say a knight, squire, peacemaker, and Baron...the last title having almost no meaning in the modern day, despite all John Farson's ranting) of the twenty-ninth generation descended from Arthur of Eld, on the side line of descent

(the long-descended get of one of Arthur's many gillies, [mistresses or prostitutes] in other words). (183-4)

King's novels are set in a fictional world with a history that largely resembles that of Earth, so while Arthur of Eld is not technically King Arthur, he is the equivalent to King Arthur in Roland's world.

King ties in the Arthurian connection later in the series when Roland has sex with a succubus so he will have a vision to help him in his quest for the Dark Tower. His semen is carried in a form of stasis inside the succubus which later takes the form of an incubus and impregnates Susannah Dean, one of Roland's companions in his quest. Later, Susannah is possessed by another succubus, Mia. Susannah's child, eventually to be born as Mordred Deschain, is transferred from Susannah to Mia's body and enters the world as a healthy baby boy, but once he nurses at Mia's breast, he reveals his demonic nature by transforming into a gigantic spider. After ripping off Mia's breast and draining her body of fluid, Mordred attempts to attack Susannah, but she uses a gun to shoot off his leg, creating a wound that never heals.

Mordred is born with an innate belief and mission that he must kill Roland Deschain so he can enter the Dark Tower where he will rule next to the Crimson King. He immediately embarks upon hunting Roland, out of jealousy of him and his friendship with his companions. Mordred even considers joining Roland's side, but he knows he cannot—his torn feelings personify the father-son conflict of Arthurian legend. Mordred is eventually killed while trying to ambush Roland and his companions. Mordred attempts to attack the sleeping Roland, but Roland manages to shoot Mordred, and his remains are then tossed into the campfire.

While the novel is not by any means a retelling of the Arthurian legend, Stephen King definitely plays with the legend's themes and creates an alternative genealogy for Arthur of Eld. In the end, King takes a traditional turn with the ending where Roland's son Mordred is destroyed, thus ending Arthur's line. The series concludes soon after this scene, and Roland is left without any children.

Bernard Cornwell also creates significant children for King Arthur in his trilogy "The Warlord Chronicles," consisting of *The Winter King* (1996), *Enemy of God* (1997), and *Excalibur* (1997). Unlike the above mentioned novelists, however, Cornwell seeks to make his novels historical, not only providing them with a setting in a grim dark age Britain, but also attempting to incorporate the Welsh traditions by recreating Arthur's sons Amhar, Loholt (a version of Llacheu) and Gwydre. The Mordred in the novels is Arthur's nephew, but he is important for he is the King of Dumnonia. Mordred's father was Arthur's deceased half-brother, also named Mordred. Arthur and the elder Mordred were both Uther's sons, but because Arthur was illegitimate, the throne has passed through the elder Mordred's line to his son. The younger Mordred is in his infancy when the trilogy opens, making Arthur one of the council who govern the British kingdom of Dumnonia for Mordred.

While these novels adopt Arthur's children from Welsh tradition, Cornwell allows the children's personalities to deviate from the characteristics attributed to them in Welsh legend. At the opening of *The Winter King*, Arthur has two bastard twin sons, Amhar and Loholt, by his mistress Ailleann. Arthur is a neglectful father, and throughout the novel the children are scarcely mentioned, appearing only on pages 108, 163, and 182. When they are mentioned, they are dismissed simply as brats. *Enemy of God* seeks to expand the role of Arthur's bastard children as well as providing Arthur with a legitimate son, Gwydre, by Arthur's marriage to Guinevere. In Welsh tradition, Amhar and Gwydre's mother is never named, while Llacheu is sometimes the son of Guinevere, so it is strange that Cornwell picks Gwydre rather than Loholt as Guinevere's son. Gwydre is significantly younger than his half-brothers who are already adults when he is born. Amhar and Loholt have now matured into wicked young men who hate their neglectful father. They become the followers of the cowardly, yet handsome, Lancelot, the exiled prince of Benoic. Lancelot eventually becomes King of the Belgic lands in Britain. Guinevere, who is hungry for power, wishes Arthur to declare himself King of Dumnonia, then unite and rule over all Britain. Arthur, however, refuses to usurp the throne from his nephew, Mordred. Seeing Arthur will never rule Britain, Guinevere turns her attention to Lancelot, becoming his lover and political supporter. Eventually, Arthur and Lancelot go to war, and Arthur's twin sons, Amhar and Loholt, side with Lancelot. Amhar and Loholt claim to be great druids who have combined ancient druidic lore with the knowledge derived from other religions such as Christianity and the Cult of Isis which have come into Britain. Merlin, however, scoffs at their claims to be druids, for the greatest magical feat the twins perform are simple tricks like pulling eggs from people's ears. During the conflict between Arthur and Lancelot, Guinevere and Gwydre become hostages in Lancelot's castle. Arthur, wishing to regain his wife and son, attacks Lancelot's strongholds, first defeating one held by Loholt. When Arthur asks the defeated Loholt how he could raise a hand against his own father, Loholt replies, "You were never a father to us" (387). Arthur then requests that Loholt place his right hand upon a stone. Loholt thinks he is about to take an oath of loyalty to his father, but instead, Arthur cuts off Loholt's hand (388), then sends Loholt to Lancelot as a warning of the approach of Arthur's army. By the novel's end, Arthur has defeated Lancelot's armies and rescued Guinevere and his son, Gwydre.

In the final novel of the series, *Excalibur*, Arthur's three children continue to have prominent roles. The novel begins with Arthur preparing to battle the Saxons. Derfel, the narrator, travels to the court of the Saxons to bargain with them. Here, he discovers Lancelot has allied himself with the Saxons, and Lancelot's supporters, Arthur's two sons, Amhar and Loholt, are also present. When peace cannot be made, the Britons and Saxons battle, culminating in Arthur's victory at Mynydd Badon. Amhar and Loholt survive the battle while Lancelot is killed. Arthur's villainous twin sons then disappear from the novel for several pages. Meanwhile, Merlin has attempted to save Briton from the Saxons by having the Old Gods return to Britain. In order to bring about the old religion's return, he must sacrifice the son of a ruler and throw the body into the Cauldron of Clyddno Eiddyn, one of the Treasures of Britain which is said to bring to life anyone who is sacrificed and thrown into it. Among Merlin's intended victims is Arthur's son, Gwydre, but Arthur rescues Gwydre before such an atrocity can be committed. As Gwydre grows up, he becomes Mordred's rival for the throne, for Mordred and his wife, Argante, have been unable to conceive a child. Gwydre marries Derfel's daughter, Morwenna, and has two children by her, a son Arthur-Bach (meaning Arthur the Little) and a daughter, Seren (298-9). Mordred, meanwhile, plots against Gwydre, by going to France and then spreading rumors that he is dying. Mordred suspects that Arthur and Derfel will now try to win the throne for Gwydre, and when they do so, he can accuse them of treason. Unaware of Mordred's plan, Derfel travels south to proclaim Gwydre's claim to the throne. Unfortunately, Derfel is captured by Mordred's forces and taken prisoner. Here he discovers that Arthur's twin sons have resurfaced as Mordred's followers. Derfel manages to escape during the night when everyone is asleep, but before he leaves the castle, he runs a blade through Amhar's neck, killing him (342). Mordred's forces now attack Arthur. Arthur does not want war, so he tries to leave Britain for Gaul, but Mordred's troops quickly attack Arthur, resulting in the Battle of Camlann. Loholt is killed in battle, and Arthur slays Mordred. Arthur and Mordred's forces are both destroyed, but as the battle ends, a neighboring king, Meurig, appears with an army to claim the right to rule Dumnonia. Arthur, Gweniver, Gwydre and Morwenna, and their children manage to escape on a fishing boat and head to France. The novel ends with Derfel watching the boat depart, and stating that no one has seen Arthur since (433).

With the end of Cornwell's trilogy, one receives the sense that Gwydre's chance of gaining the throne is now hopeless. Arthur's family, however, may live on in Gaul, where Gwydre's children will marry and multiply, thus continuing Arthur's bloodline.

Stephen Lawhead's *Avalon: The Return of King Arthur* (1999) is the first novel to bring the descent of Arthur's children down to the present day. This novel was a follow-up to Lawhead's popular Pendragon Cycle: *Taliesin* (1987), *Merlin* (1988), *Arthur* (1989), *Pendragon* (1994), and *Grail* (1997). While the Pendragon Cycle

novels are set in Arthurian times, *Avalon* brings about the return of
King Arthur in a modern day. Besides including a descendant of
King Arthur, it's one of the few books, Susan Cooper's last volume
of "The Dark Is Rising" series, *Silver on the Tree* (1977) being
another, to bring about King Arthur's return. While readers are
bound to be a bit disappointed by the ending—it's almost
impossible for Arthur to return and not make it disappointing—the
novel is engrossing.

The main character, Captain James Arthur Stuart, is, unknown
to him, a descendant of King Arthur via the Stuart monarchy. When
King Edward IX of England dies, the prime minister tries to get all
heirs to the throne to abdicate. Then James, who is not only
Arthur's descendant, but King Arthur reincarnated, claims the
throne as King Arthur II. Besides the political factions against his
reign, evil magical forces are seeking to bring about King Arthur II's
destruction which all leads to the climactic discovery of the lost
Avalon.

In 2003, Elizabeth Wein, author of *The Winter Prince*, returned
to her Arthurian stories by giving the tale one of the strangest twists
of any author when she had King Arthur's children, Goewin and
Medraut, along with Medraut's children, living in Ethiopia.

In the first novel, *A Coalition of Lions* (2003), it is six years after
Medraut returned from Aksum (Ethiopia) and a "bare season" after
he and Lleu nearly killed each other. Camlann has just been fought.
Mordred causes the battle by slaying an adder, but he is fighting
with Arthur against Cynric of the West Saxons. Mordred ultimately
slays Arthur at his father's request. Lleu also dies in battle. Mordred
then disappears, leaving Lleu's twin sister, Goewin, to seek
protection. She flees from Mordred's mother Morgause who would
turn her over as bounty to Cynric, who wants to marry Goewin to
one of his grandsons.

Goewin flees Britain with the help of Priamos, the ambassador to
Britain from Aksum. Together they escape to Aksum where her
cousin, Constantine, is currently ambassador, having replaced
Medraut in that role. Once in Aksum, Goewin learns that Medraut
has a son, Telemakos, by Turunesh, the daughter of Kidane, a royal

counselor and relative of the emperor. Goewin has a struggle with Constantine over the throne, using Telemakos as a pawn because she claims he has more right to the throne than Constantine, despite Telemakos' father Medraut being illegitimate. Ultimately, it is discovered Medraut has also made his way to Aksum, and peace is made with Constantine, resulting in it being agreed that he will return to Britain to make peace with Cynric and be the new King of Britain. Goewin, Medraut, and Telemakos remain in Aksum and play roles at the court. Goewin becomes Britain's ambassador to Aksum since Constantine has left. Priamos also returns to Britain to be Aksum's ambassador there, and although there is a sense that Priamos and Goewin feel love for each other, they do not unite in the future novels.

The rest of the sequels are involved with politics and intrigue in the Aksum court and have little to do with Britain itself. Telemakos becomes the focus of the novels as a boy who has some extraordinary adventures and plays a part, often behind the scenes or through stealth, in the political manipulations. In *The Sunbird* (2004), Medraut and Turunesh conceive another child who is born in *The Lion Killer* (2007) and given the name Athena. In the next novel, *The Empty Kingdom* (2008), Athena reaches the age of three. Telemakos, as the result of a plague that kills Constantine's children, finds out he has been named heir to Constantine, which suggests Arthur's descendants will again sit on Britain's throne, but this event occurs near the end of the novel.

Following the publication of *The Empty Kingdom,* Elizabeth Wein revealed in an interview that she is working on a story told from Athena's point of view as a twelve year old. Other than suggesting Athena might become a "vet" (veterinarian) no further clues were provided as to what this novel might contain. It remains to be seen whether Wein will have Telemakos return to Britain to inherit his grandfather King Artos' throne.

Wein has painstakingly tried to portray Ethiopian history accurately, and while readers have to wonder why she decided to introduce Ethiopia as the home of Arthur's children and grandchildren, she does note in the "Author's Note" to *A Coalition of Lions* that Malory first introduced in *Le Morte D'Arthur* the son of an African prince named Priamus, who battles Sir Gawain, is wounded, converted to Christianity, and eventually knighted as one of the companions of the Round Table in the same section where Constantine is named Arthur's heir. She goes on to add that if Britain and Ethiopia did not have connections in Arthurian times, then why was a sixth century Aksumite coin found in Hastings in South England, and why do the silver pennies of eighth century British King Offa resemble it? (Wein, *Coalition*, 201-3).

The same year Wein began her sequels to *The Winter Prince*, Debra Kemp took the idea of King Arthur's daughter to new lengths by beginning her *The House of Pendragon* series. So far, two of the three novels of the series have been published, *The Firebrand* (2003) and *The Recruit* (2007).

While Vera Chapman's *King Arthur's Daughter* first covered this territory, Kemp is far more detailed in her imagining of a daughter for Arthur. Some of the first novel's suspense is lost because we know from the back cover, and the frame of the novel, that Lin is King Arthur's daughter, although she does not know this herself. Lin was kidnapped at an early age by Arthur's sister, Morgause, and it was believed the boat she was on, enroute to the Orkney Isles, had sunk and she had died. Actually, Morgause had taken her to Orkney and made her a slave. Lin grows up believing she is the daughter of a slave woman, and except for the kindness of her foster-brother David and a few of the other slaves, she knows a life of relentless hardship. When Prince Modred decides specifically to torture her and make her his plaything, her life becomes nearly unbearable, yet Lin is of iron nature, so she refuses to give up until finally she learns the truth of her heritage.

Debra Kemp continues the story of Princess Lin in *The Recruit*. Here Lin comes to Camelot to find she is expected by her mother, Guinevere, to act like the perfect lady, learning to sew, and to prepare herself for a dynastic marriage that will provide stability to the kingdom. Lin will have none of it. After some initial struggles with her mother, Lin convinces her father, King Arthur, to let her join the army. She becomes "the recruit" and proves herself capable of serving as well as any man in the army. From barroom brawls to guard duty, Lin continually proves herself as worthy of her sire.

What I actually find most interesting about these two novels is the frame that surrounds them. Kemp begins the first novel with Lin speaking just after the Battle of Camlann and the death of Arthur and Modred. There is no prophecy here that Arthur will come again, but rather Lin pretends Arthur will return to keep up the hope of the people. Then the book shifts forward a number of years; Lin is married to Gaheris and has been raising her family, not revealing to her own children that they are the Pendragon's grandchildren. She has journeyed back to Camelot now and is considering taking back reign over the kingdom. It is then that she tells her story to her oldest son, technically named Arthur, but called Bear by the family. She tells her son of her days as a slave in Orkney and how she found out she is King Arthur's daughter. The frame also makes it clear that Lin will become a great warrior.

Kemp is currently working on the third and final volume of the series. I am curious whether, besides depicting the events that lead up to the fall of Camelot and the Battle of Camlann, Kemp will show Lin's life in more detail after the Battle of Camlann—will Lin establish a united kingdom again? Will the story of Camelot have a new ending?

In 2008, Jessica Bonito published *Camelot Lost*, which makes Arthur's Welsh son Amr a major character. In the novel, Arthur is High King and married to Guinivere. He has successfully held back the Saxons and his reign is prosperous until his old lover Morgaine shows up at Camelot with their son, Amr. Arthur wants Amr's parentage kept secret, but he acknowledges Morgaine as his sister and Amr as his nephew. Only after Arthur and Morgaine sleep together again do they find out they truly are siblings. Arthur banishes Morgaine forever from Camelot, so she returns to Avalon where she gives birth to Mordred. Years later, as Morgaine dies, she begs Mordred to go to Camelot to claim his birthright.

Mordred journeys to Camelot, along with Morgain's priestess friend Morgause and her son Everarde. Once at Camelot, Mordred and Guinivere immediately develop feelings for each other. At first,

Guinivere resists, but when Arthur, upon learning Morgaine is dead, confesses to Guinivere that Morgaine is the woman he has loved the most, Guinivere is driven into Mordred's arms.

Amr and Mordred, having forged an alliance through brotherly bonds, begin to plot against Arthur and wield charms that summon the apparition of their mother to torture him. Eventually, the Knights of the Round Table learn of Arthur's incestuous affair, and after Amr and Mordred arrange the death of Everarde at Arthur's hands, Arthur loses the loyalty of his men. Then when Arthur's best friend, Sir Constantine, turns against him, calling him a traitor to Britain, Arthur is banished from Britain while Mordred is crowned High King and marries Guinivere.

As the years pass, Arthur learns that Mordred and Guinivere have two sons, Melehan and Melou, who after training in the arts of war and magic in Avalon, are now Knights of the Round Table. In rage at Mordred and his family's happiness, Arthur makes alliances with the Saxons to exact his revenge. In time, word spreads that a new Saxon warlord is in Britain. Amr and Sir Constantine journey to the warlord's lands where they learn the warlord is Arthur.

Arthur now begins his revenge by convincing Constantine to join his army, after he reveals to him Mordred and Amr's sins. Merlyn, Avalon's sorcerer, appears to endorse Arthur's plans, but in fact, Merlyn is Morgause in disguise. She is furious at the death of her son Everarde, and at Amr and Mordred's role in it. She is now determined to destroy all of the Pendragon line.

The battle of Camlann follows where Arthur and Mordred fight one another. Mordred is wounded by an arrow from Constantine and Arthur cuts off Mordred's hand, but Guinivere then appears, and grabbing Mordred's sword, she strikes Arthur.

Guinivere and her sons now rush Mordred to the shore, hoping to take him to Avalon to be restored. However, Constantine follows them and slays Melehan and Melou. Morgause, still in the guise of Merlyn, appears and kills Constantine, but then her disguise melts away and Guinivere slays her. Guinivere and Mordred then set sail toward Avalon, but before they can reach it, Mordred dies in her arms.

After days of Guinivere being in grief and shock, Merlyn appears and takes her to Avalon where she gives birth to a daughter, Adela. The novel closes with Guinivere gazing from Avalon's shore toward Camelot.

Along with Bernard Cornwell, Jessica Bonito has definitely done the most to introduce the Welsh children back into the story, even if only the one child Amr. She also does more than any previous novelist to depict Mordred's children traditionally. Interestingly, however, it is a completely new child, Adela, who is the only one left alive at the novel's end. Arthur's line continues through Mordred and Guinivere's daughter, although Adela seems unlikely to reclaim Arthur's throne.

Finally, I wish to note my own upcoming novel *King Arthur's Legacy*, which will also focus upon descendants of King Arthur. While I won't give away the plot here, it's sufficient to say that it really predates many of the novels discussed here. I initially started writing it in 1993, and when I realized how much research into the Arthurian legend I would need to do, I decided to use that research not only for my novel but also as the basis of my Master's Thesis on the topic of King Arthur's children, which became the early version of this book. After completing my M.A. Thesis and then the draft of *King Arthur's Legacy*, I became sidetracked with writing my other novels, starting with *The Marquette Trilogy*. I put the Arthurian legend on the back burner, other than writing an article "King Arthur's Children: A Trend in Modern Fiction" in the journal *Arthuriana* in 1999. Recently, I have extensively revised *King Arthur's Legacy* and hope to publish it in the next couple of years and turn it into a series that will trace Arthur's descendants down to the twenty-first century. I promise to provide many twists and turns to the legend, including insight into King Arthur, Mordred, Constantine, and Morgan le Fay as some of the major characters. Arthur and Guinevere will be the parents of the Welsh children, Gwydre and Llacheu, and Mordred's sons will also be of consequence to the storyline.

In my M.A. Thesis, which I completed in 1995, and again in the 1999 *Arthuriana* article, I predicted that authors would continue to create fiction that includes more children for King Arthur. I have apparently been correct in that prediction.

The interest by modern novelists in creating new children for King Arthur suggests an effort to change the legend's traditional ending to provide Arthur with heirs, rather than leaving him without a successor after his and Mordred's deaths at the Battle of Camlann. Several novelists have allowed newly-created children to take on major roles in Arthurian novels, creating a less tragic ending to the legend, as well as providing the possibility of a genealogical link between Arthur and future generations even into the twenty-first century. If future novelists continue to create children for King Arthur, we may witness the legend evolve into a story with a less tragic outcome. Such an evolution is only natural to a story which has continually changed and adapted to each new period, whether to allow Malory to comment upon the Wars of the Roses or Mark Twain to mock his own capitalistic nineteenth century. The Arthurian legend has always tried to stretch beyond any boundaries writers have set for it, preventing its becoming stagnant or merely a literary curiosity. Continual additions and subtractions to the legend have been made over the centuries, including the deletion of Arthur's Welsh children from the stories, the introduction of Lancelot by the French romancers, and the transformation of Mordred from Arthur's nephew to his bastard son born in incest. It is impossible to say what will be the effect if novelists continue to create children for Arthur. Undoubtedly, the legend will only keep evolving and renewing itself for future generations as it has for the last thousand years.

The modern novels I have discussed often represent a Camelot in contrast to our confusing, technological, fast-paced modern world, a Camelot where life is envisioned as a simpler or more ideal time to which we long to return. Several of these novels also depict Camelot as a kingdom before its time, one where women could have major roles, a feminist way of retelling the legend to connect the Arthurian world to our own, as seen by the number of daughters created for King Arthur. By creating Arthurian descendants, many novelists leave open the possibility that these descendants may yet live among us. If novelists continue to make this connection between the present and the Arthurian era, not only may our modern age come to feel a little closer to the age of Camelot, but the increase in the significance of Arthur's children may transform the legend from its tragic endings to a story with a much different conclusion, and perhaps as a consequence, with a much different meaning than the tragic emphasis upon destiny and fate which it has traditionally contained.

Conclusion

What then can we conclude about King Arthur's children? Did they ever exist? Scholars are more convinced today than at any other time in Arthurian studies that some historical figure lived who became the basis for King Arthur, whether he was Riothamus, as Geoffrey Ashe believes, or some other type of warrior chief. If King Arthur did live, then it is just as possible that he had children. The Welsh children, Llacheu, Gwydre, and Amr are probably the closest we will ever come to knowing whether Arthur actually had any children. In the last fifteen hundred years, so many liberties have been taken with the subject of King Arthur's children that we must look hard and perhaps forever to find the truth behind them. We might even decide it hardly matters whether Arthur really had any children since writers have invented them whenever they wished, ignoring or digressing from traditions that might have some basis in historical truth.

The historical basis of King Arthur's children became convoluted with the disappearance of the Welsh children from later Arthurian works. This disappearance is largely the result of Geoffrey of Monmouth's decision that the plot would be more dramatic if Arthur had no heirs other than Mordred and if Arthur and Mordred both died. Geoffrey of Monmouth also made Guinevere barren so Arthur would have no heir, making the reader more sympathetic toward him. The lack of an heir allowed Geoffrey of Monmouth and his successors to cause the downfall of the kingdom which is more dramatic than a simple passing of the crown from a monarch to his successor. The success of these changes in the plot made Geoffrey of Monmouth's retelling of the Arthurian legend become the definitive version for at least three centuries until Sir Thomas Malory wrote his *Le Morte D'Arthur.*

Geoffrey's successors in the Middle Ages followed his concept that Arthur had no children with the exception of Mordred. Occasionally, as we have seen, a writer invented children for Arthur, without any basis in the Arthurian tradition, but these writers had no significant influence upon later Arthurian tradition because Geoffrey of Monmouth had shaped the plot around Arthur's lack of an heir. If a writer invented children for Arthur, a way had to be found for these children to die before Arthur's death, or else the Arthurian tradition had to be completely rewritten, a daunting task which made it easier to exclude the possibility of Arthur having any children other than Mordred.

It has only been in modern times, with an overwhelming new interest in Arthurian literature, particularly among late twentieth and early twenty-first century writers of fantasy, that Arthur's children have made a noticeable reappearance. The modern writers who introduce these new children of Arthur usually have some knowledge of Geoffrey of Monmouth or Sir Thomas Malory, but they are rarely scholars of the legend and have either forgotten, are ignorant of, or chose to disregard the existence of the early Welsh children attributed to Arthur. The Welsh children are probably inconvenient, due to their deaths prior to Arthur's own, to modern novelists who are seeking to connect the present to the Arthurian world; authors like Vera Chapman and Susan Cooper have tried to make this connection through a continuum of Arthur's bloodline down to the present day. Since Welsh tradition states that Llacheu, Amr, and Gwydre all died prior to their father, they can become little more than subplots in the larger plot of Arthurian fantasy unless some modern writer wished to dispute their deaths, or state that they had children before they died, which no writer has yet done. Writers have preferred, rather than following earlier traditions, to create new sons and daughters for Arthur.

The sudden reemergence of interest in King Arthur's children may be connected with Geoffrey Ashe's comments about Americans and their fascination with "roots" as already discussed in the

Introduction. The subject of history has never before been as unfolded to the masses as it has in recent years when we can get a history lesson everytime we turn on the television and the Internet allows anyone to retell history as he or she sees fit on a personal website. Technology is shrinking the centuries between us and King Arthur. As we become more familiar with the past, we wonder what our own historical origins are, which has led to an increased interest in genealogy, now the third most popular hobby in the United States.

The creation of genealogies has always been important in Arthurian literature. Genealogies were used by Arthurian writers to make King Arthur a descendant of the Roman Emperor Maximus and to make the Grail family the descendants of Joseph of Arimathea. Of specific interest to our study, as we have seen, are the probably fictional creation of genealogies that attempt to connect the British royal family and the Campbell Clan of Scotland to King Arthur. For modern writers, creating genealogies that credit King Arthur with descendants attempts to make the Arthurian legend seem more realistic as history. If our storytellers write that King Arthur had children, and that his descendants are living among us today, then we become more willing to believe that King Arthur once existed as a historical person. Similarly, our belief that King Arthur once lived makes us want to believe his descendants are living today and perhaps that we are among those descendants.

Whether King Arthur had children will probably never be known, but the possibility is open enough that lovers of Arthurian literature can secretly believe they are his descendants. Vera Chapman writes that "Nobody can say that King Arthur did *not* have a daughter" (7). Neither can anyone claim that King Arthur's descendants have not multiplied all over the world by the twenty-first century.

Ultimately, whether or not King Arthur's blood does flow in one's veins today, it is not necessary for a person to be King Arthur's descendant. Everyone who loves Arthurian literature is a child of King Arthur. The tales of King Arthur have been handed down from one generation to the next for fifteen centuries, both in written and oral form. When these stories are told, they take up a permanent place in the human heart and become part of mankind's story, giving meaning to our lives and inspiring us to create a better world, just as King Arthur tried to do at Camelot. This dream of a golden age is our inheritance from King Arthur, and as long as we have this dream, we will be carrying out King Arthur's legacy, and King Arthur will live among us.

Appendix: Mordred and Modron

Before we leave Mordred, we should notice that there may be some confusion between him as either Arthur's son or brother, and between Mordred and a brother of Arthur's named Modron. The confusion is further increased since Modron usually appears as Arthur's sister rather than brother.

R.S. Loomis tells us that the ravens of *The Mabinogion* who battle with Arthur's knights are Arthur's nephew Owain's mother, Modron, and her sisters, the daughters of Avallach (*Wales* 96-7). Loomis also states that Morgan le Fay and Modron have a connection because both are daughters of Avallach (*Celtic Myth* 192). If Morgan le Fay and Modron are sisters, we must first wonder whether they are Arthur's sisters, making them the daughters of one of Arthur's parents, or are they the children of Avallach? If Modron is Owain's mother, it seems strange that Morgan is also frequently credited with having a child named Owain. Perhaps the two are not sisters, but merely the same person with a confused identity. This situation may be a similar case to Arthur's Welsh sons becoming confused or integrated into Mordred.

Celtic scholars are in agreement that Modron, who seems to be Morgan le Fay's sister, is the old Gallo-Roman goddess Matrona, who gave her name to the river Marne, and therefore, seems to be connected with water (Loomis, *Celtic Myth*, 193). If this connection to a river is true, it should not surprise us that Modron is sister to Morgan, who is often the Lady of the Lake.

When the Welsh wrote of Modron in their legends, they made her the mother of both Owain and Mabon (Loomis, *Celtic Myth*, 193). This son, Mabon, can be traced back to Apollo Maponos, who was worshiped in both Gaul and Britain (Loomis, *Celtic Myth*, 4).

What is strange is that if Modron were a female, she should later appear as Arthur's brother in a modern novel such as in Edward Franklin's *The Bear of Britain* (1944), where he is treacherous, along with Mordred, who is here Arthur's nephew (Thompson 41).

In other works, Mordred has been depicted as Arthur's brother, which may be another confusion with Modron, but more likely authors just taking license with the story. In Edison Marshall's novel *The Pagan King* (1959), Mordred is Arthur's half-brother. Why would Arthur have both a treacherous brother and nephew? In Marshall's opinion, it must have seemed easier to combine the two into one character. We may then wonder whether Mordred and Modron have an older mythological connection or at least these writers are drawing upon what they want to believe is a lost connection.

In the *Prince Valiant* comic strip, begun by Hal Foster in 1937 and still running in more than 300 newspapers each Sunday, Mordred is also Arthur's half-brother. In this case Mordred has a daughter, but she is not King Arthur's direct descendant as a result. Mordred's daughter Maeve marries Arn, the son of Prince Valiant. Arn and Maeve's daughter Ingrid (born in the 1987 comic strip) has been designated as Arthur's heir. Mordred has been removed from the line of succession. My guess is that Foster chose to depict Mordred as Arthur's half-brother to avoid the issue of incest in a comic strip; I doubt Foster was interested in the relationship between Mordred and Modron.

Modron cannot be readily accepted as an early brother of Arthur. Nowhere in early traditions does he appear as such. However, in Welsh tradition is a tale where Arthur speaks to an eagle, which reveals itself to be his deceased nephew, Elewlod, the son of Madawg, son of Uthr (Bromwich, *Arthur Welsh*, 58). That Madawg's son should become an eagle, may remind us of Modron as a raven, and also the legends which tell of Arthur being turned into a raven rather than dying. Perhaps then we can accept Madawg as being Modron.

Modron's reasons for becoming confused with Mordred may also have explanations. We have seen Modron's possibility as a sister to Morgan le Fay, Lady of the Lake. Modron herself is connected to river goddesses. Mordred definitely has a connection to water through his mythological ancestor, Dylan. Suggested connections have also been made betwen Pryderi and Rhiannon and Modron and Mabon, who was also taken away when three nights old from his mother (MacCana 83). In "Culhwch and Olwen," Cei and Gwrhyr search for Mabon and must ask all the oldest animals where he may be. In her chapter "Chrétien de Troyes," Jean Frappier points out that in *Yvain* are blended in traditions of Modron as a water nymph (Loomis, *Arthurian Literature*,163), and in an Irish tale, a character named Fraech is wounded by a water-monster and is then carried away by his fairy kinswomen to be healed. In her chapter "The Vulgate Cycle," Jean Frappier makes notice of another Irish tale that tells of Fergus mac Leite being wounded by a water-monster, and as he lays by the lake dying, he charges his people that his sword Caladcolg (the original of Excalibur) should be preserved till it can be given to a fitting lord (Loomis, *Arthurian Literature*, 310). Could Mordred then have an origin as a water monster or as a female goddess of the sea? Or could there be a lost tradition that Mordred is the son of Modron? Why not, since we already have Morgan le Fay and Morgause as possible mothers for him.

Accurate connections between Mordred and Modron have not yet been made, but the similarities may point to a need for further investigation into this matter.

Bibliography

Adventures of Orlando and Melora, The. In *The Book of Arthur: Lost Tales of the Round Table*. Ed. John Matthews. Old Saybrook, CT: Konecky & Konecky, 2002. 46-60.

A Kid in King Arthur's Court. Dir. Michael Gottlieb. With Thomas Ian Nicholas, Joss Ackland, and Art Malik. Walt Disney, 1995.

Annales Cambriae. Ed. John Willems Ab Ithel. London: Longman, Green, Longman, and Roberts, 1860, microcard.

Ancestral File. Computer software. Church of Jesus Christ of Latter Day Saints, 1992.

Anglo-Saxon Chronicle, The. Ed. and trans. G.N. Garmonsway. 1953. London, Gr. Brit.: J.M. Dent Ltd., 1992.

Ashe, Geoffrey. *The Discovery of King Arthur*. London, Gr. Brit.: Guild Publishing, 1985.

Blaess, Madeleine. "Arthur's Sisters." *Bulletin Bibliographique de la Societe Internationale Arthurienne*. 8 (1956): 69-77.

Bonito, Jessica. *Camelot Lost*. Frederick, MD: PublishAmerica, 2008.

Boughton, Rutland. "King Arthur had Three Sons." *The Barkshire Tragedy and King Arthur had Three Sons*. London: Novello & Co., Ltd., n.d.

Bradley, Marion Zimmer. *The Mists of Avalon*. 1982. New York: Ballantine Books, May 1984.

Bromwich, Rachel, A.O.H. Jarman, and Brynley F. Roberts eds. *The Arthur of the Welsh: The Arthurian Legend in Medieval Welsh Literature*. Cardiff: University of Wales Press, 1991.

Bruce, J.D. "Arthuriana." *The Romanic Review*. 3 (1912): 173-93.

Bruce, J.D. *Evolution of the Arthurian Romance*. 2 vols. Gloucester, MS: Peter Smith, 1958.

Camelot. Dir. Moss Hart. With Richard Harris, Vanessa Redgrave, Franco Nero, David Hemmings, and Lionel Jeffries. Warner Bros., 1967.

Campbell, Joseph. *The Masks of God: Occidental Mythology*. 1964. New York: Penguin Books, 1976.

Chapman, Vera. *King Arthur's Daughter*. 1976. New York: Avon Books, June 1978.

Christian, Catherine. *The Pendragon*. New York: Warner Books, 1978.

Cooper, Susan. *The Grey King*. New York: Athenum, February 1976.

Cooper, Susan. *Silver on the Tree*. New York: Athenum, 1977.

Cowan, Thomas. *Fire in the Head: Shamanism and the Celtic Spirit*. San Francisco: Harper Collins Publishers, 1993.

Cornwell, Bernard. *The Winter King*. New York: St. Martin's Press, 1996.

Cornwell, Bernard. *Enemy of God*. New York: St. Martin's Press, 1997.

Cornwell, Bernard. *Excalibur*. London, Gr. Brit.: Michael Joseph, 1997.

Crompton, Anne Eliot. *Merlin's Harp*. New York: Penguin, 1997.

Cross, Tom Peete. "The Celtic Elements in the Lays of *Lanval* and *Graelent*." *Modern Philogy*: 12. 10 (1915): 585-644.

Evans, Sebastian trans. *The High History of the Holy Graal*. 1910. New York: E.P. Dutton & Co., 1929.

Faces of America with Henry Louis Gates, Jr. Episode 4: "Know Thyself." Dir./Producer Stephen Ives and Amanda Pollak. With Elizabeth Alexander, Stephen Colbert, Eva Longoria, Meryl Streep et al. PBS, 2010.

Fielding, Henry. *The Tragedy of Tragedies; or the Life and Death of Tom Thumb the Great*. 1731. *Eighteenth Century English Literature*. eds. Geoffrey Tillotson et al. New York: Harcourt, Brace & World Inc., 1969. 729-56.

Fletcher, Robert Huntington. *The Arthurian Materials in the Chronicles Especially Those of Great Britain and France*. New York: Haskell House, 1965.

Frappier, Jean. "Chretien de Troyes." *Arthurian Literature in the Middle Ages: A Collaborative History*. ed. R.S. Loomis 1959. Oxford, Gr. Brit.: Clarendon Press, 1974. 157-91.

Frappier, Jean. "The Vulgate Cycle." *Arthurian Literature in the Middle Ages: A Collaborative History*. ed. R.S. Loomis. 1959. Oxford, Gr. Brit.: Clarendon Press, 1974. 295-318.

Gardner, Laurence. *The Illustrated Bloodline of the Holy Grail: The Hidden Lineage of Jesus Revealed*. New York: Barnes & Noble, 2000.

Geoffrey of Monmouth. *The History of the Kings of Britain*. Trans. Lewis Thorpe. London, Gr. Brit.: Penguin Books, 1966.

Geoffrey of Monmouth. *Vita Merlini*. Trans. John Jay Parry. Illinois: U of Illinois P, 1925.

Gildas. *The Works of Gildas. Six Old English Chronicles*. Ed. J.A. Giles. 1848. New York: AMS Press, 1968.

Godwin, Parke. *Firelord*. 1980. New York: Avon Books, 1994.

Godwin, Parke. *Beloved Exile*. 1984. New York: Avon Books, 1994.

Goodrich, Norma Lorre. *Guinevere*. New York: Harper Collins Publishers, 1991.

Goodrich, Norma Lorre. *King Arthur*. New York: Franklin Watts, 1986.

Goodrich, Norma Lorre. *Merlin*. New York: Franklin Watts, 1987.

Goodrich, Norma Lorre. *The Holy Grail*. 1992. New York: Harper Perennial, 1993.

Guinevere. Dir. Jud Taylor. With Sheryl Lee and Sean Patrick Flannery. Lifetime, 1994.

Hovey, Richard. *The Birth of Galahad.* 1898. New York: Duffield and Company, 1909.

Jones, Mary J. *Avalon.* Tallahassee, FL: Naiad Press, 1991.

Kemp, Debra A. *The House of Pendragon Book I: The Firebrand.* n.p.: Amber Quill Press, 2003.

Kemp, Debra A. *The House of Pendragon Book II: The Recruit.* n.p.: Amber Quill Press, 2007.

Kennealy-Morrison, Patricia. *The Copper Crown.* New York: Roc-Penguin, 1986.

Kennealy-Morrison, Patricia. *The Throne of Scone.* New York: Roc-Penguin, 1987.

Kennealy-Morrison, Patricia. *The Silver Branch.* New York: Roc-Penguin, 1989.

Kennealy-Morrison, Patricia. *The Hawk's Gray Feather.* New York: Harper Collins, 1990.

Kennealy-Morrison, Patricia. *The Oak Above the Kings.* New York: Roc-Penguin, 1995.

Kennealy-Morrison, Patricia. *The Hedge of Mist.* New York: Harper Collins, 1996.

King, Stephen. *The Dark Tower: The Dark Tower VII.* Hampton Falls, NH: Donald M. Grant, 2004.

King, Stephen. *Song of Susannah: The Dark Tower VI.* Hampton Falls, NH: Donald M. Grant, 2004.

King, Stephen. *Wizard and Glass: The Dark Tower IV.* New York: Plume, 1997.

Lacy, Norris J. et al., eds. *The Arthurian Encyclopedia.* New York and London: Garland Publishing, Inc., 1986.

Lacy, Norris J. and Geoffrey Ashe. *The Arthurian Handbook.* New York and London: Garland Publishing, Inc., 1988.

Lawhead, Stephen. *Avalon: The Return of King Arthur.* New York: Avon Books, 1999.

Layamon. Brut. *Arthurian Chronicles represented by Wace and Layamon.* London, Gr. Brit.: J.M. Dent and Sons Ltd, n.d.

Le Mort D'Arthur: The Legend of a King. Narr. Donald Sutherland. Writ. Dale Minor. Prod. Dale Minor and Linda Duvoisin. *Great Books.* The Learning Channel. Discovery Communications Inc., 1993.

Loomis, Roger Sherman ed. *Arthurian Literature in the Middle Ages: A Collaborative History.* 1959. Oxford, Gr.Brit.: Clarendon Press, 1974.

Loomis, Roger Sherman. *Celtic Myth and Arthurian Romance.* 1927. New York: Haskell House Publishers Ltd., 1967.

Loomis, Roger Sherman. *Wales and the Arthurian Legend.* Folcroft, PA: The Folcroft Press, Inc., 1969.

Mabinogion, The. Trans. Lady Charlotte Guest. New York: E.P. Dutton & Co., March 1913 reprint.

Mabinogion, The. Trans. Gwyn and Thomas Jones. Rutland, VT: Charles E. Tuttle Co., Inc., 1992.

MacCana, Proinsias. *Celtic Mythology.* New York: Hamlyn Publishing Group Limited, 1970.

MacCulloch, J.A. *Mythology of All Races.* vol. 3 of 13. 1917. New York: Cooper Square Publishers, Inc., 1964.

Malmesbury, William of. *Chronicle of the Kings of England.* ed. J.A. Giles. 1847. New York: AMS Press, 1968.

Malory, Sir Thomas. *Le Morte D'Arthur.* vol. 2 of 2. ed. Janet Cowen. London, Gr. Brit.: Penguin Books, 1969.

Matthews, Caitlin and John. *The Arthurian Book of Days.* New York: Macmillan Publishing Company, 1990.

Matthews, John. *King Arthur's Britain: A Photographic Odyssey.* London, Gr. Brit.: Blandford, 1995.

Matthews, John. "Notes: The Adventures of Melora and Orlando." *The Book of Arthur: Lost Tales of the Round Table.* Ed. John Matthews. Old Saybrook, CT: Konecky & Konecky, 2002. 379-80.

McKenzie, Nancy. *The High Queen*. New York: Del Rey, 1995.

Merriman, James Douglas. *The Flower of Kings: A Study of the Arthurian Legend in England Between 1485 and 1835*. Lawrence, KS: University Press of Kansas, 1973.

Moncreiffe, Sir Iain of that Ilk. *Royal Highness*. London, Gr. Brit.: H. Hamilton, 1982.

Nennius. *History of the Britons. Six Old English Chronicles*. Ed. J.A. Giles. 1848. New York: AMS Press, 1968.

Newstead, Helaine. *Bran the Blessed in Arthurian Romance*. Morningside Heights, New York: Columbia University Press, 1939.

Norgate, Kate. *John Lackland*. 1902. New York: AMS Press, 1970.

Olson, Steve. *Mapping Human History: Discovering the Past Through Our Genes*. New York: Houghton Mifflin, 2002.

Painter, Sidney. *The Reign of King John*. 1949. Baltimore, MD: The John Hopkins Press, 1959.

Parry, John J. and Robert A. Caldwell. "Geoffrey of Monmouth." *Arthurian Literature in the Middle Ages: A Collaborative History*. ed. R.S. Loomis. 1959. Oxford, Gr. Brit.: Clarendon Press, 1974. 72-93.

Paton, Lucy Allen. *Studies in the Fairy Mythology of Arthurian Romance*. 2nd ed. New York: Burt Franklin, 1970.

Rhys, John. *Celtic Folklore: Welsh and Manx*. 1901. New York: Benjamin Blom, Inc., 1972.

Rhys, John. *Studies in the Arthurian Legend*. Oxford, Gr. Brit.: Clarendon Press, 1891.

Rolleston, T.W. *Celtic Myths and Legends*. 1911. Orig. Title: *Myths and Legends of the Celtic Race*. New York: Dover Publications, Inc., 1990.

Sellar, W.D.H. "The Earliest Campbells—Norman, Briton or Gael?" *Scottish Studies*. vol. 17, no. 2 (1973): 109-25.

Stewart, Mary. *The Wicked Day.* 1983. New York: Fawcett Crest, September, 1984.

Stewart, William. *The buik of the cronicles of Scotland, or A metrical version of the history of Hector Boece.* ed. William B. Turnbull. London, Gr. Brit.: Longman, Brown, Green, Longmans, and Roberts, 1858.

Sutcliff, Rosemary. *Sword at Sunset.* New York: Coward-McCann, Inc., 1963.

Tatlock, J.S.P. *The Legendary History of Britain: Geoffrey of Monmouth's Historia Regum Britanniae and Its Early Vernacular Versions.* Berkeley and Los Angeles: University of California Press, 1950.

Thomas Urquhart. Wikipedia. http://en.wikipedia.org/wiki/Thomas_Urquhart Accessed March 29, 2010.

Thompson, Raymond H. *The Return from Avalon: A Study of the Arthurian Legend in Modern Fiction.* Westport, CT: Greenwood Press, 1985.

Thiðrekssaga. In *Legends of the Middle Ages: Narrated with Special Reference to Literature and Art.* Ed. H.A. Guerber. 1896. Kindle Edition, March 17, 2006.

Tichelaar, Tyler R. "King Arthur's Children: A Trend in Modern Fiction." *Arthuriana* vol. 9 no. 2 (1999): 39-56.

Tichelaar, Tyler R. *King Arthur's Children in Fiction and Tradition.* M.A. Thesis. Marquette, MI: Northern Michigan University, 1995.

Troyes, Chrétien de. *Lancelot or, The Knight of the Cart (Le Chevalier de la Charrete).* ed. and trans. William W. Kibler. New York: Garland Publishing, Inc., 1981.

Urquhart, Thomas. *The Works of Sir Thomas Urquhart of Cromarty, Knight.* Edinburgh, Gr. Brit.: H. and J. Pillans, 1834.

Viscardi, Antonio. "Arthurian Influences on Italian Literature: From 1200 to 1500." *Arthurian Literature in the Middle*

Ages: A Collaborative History. ed. R.S. Loomis. 1959. Oxford, Gr. Brit: Clarendon Press, 1974. 419-29.

Von Zatzikhoven, Ulrich. *Lanzelet.* Trans. Kenneth G.T. Webster. Revised by Roger Sherman Loomis. New York: Columbia University Press, 1951.

Wace. *Roman de Brut. Arthurian Chronicles represented by Wace and Brut.* London: J.M. Dent and Sons, Ltd, n.d.

Wein, Elizabeth C. *The Winter Prince.* New York: Atheneum, 1993.

Wein, Elizabeth C. *A Coalition of Lions.* New York: Viking, 2003.

Wein, Elizabeth C. *The Sunbird.* New York: Viking, 2004.

Wein, Elizabeth C. *The Lion Hunter: The Mark of Solomon ~ Book One.* New York: Viking, 2007.

Wein, Elizabeth C. *The Empty Kingdom: The Mark of Solomon ~ Book Two.* New York: Viking, 2008.

Wein, Elizabeth C. Interview.

http://writingya.blogspot.com/2008/11/wbbt-elizabeth-e-wein.html Accessed March 21, 2010.

Westwood, Jennifer. *Albion: A Guide to Legendary Britain.* 1985. London, Gr. Brit.: Grafton, 1992.

Wolf, Joan. *The Road to Avalon.* 1988. New York: Onyx Books, September 1989.

Wolfram von Eschenbach. *Parzival.* Trans. Edwin H. Zeydel. Chapel Hill, N.C.: University of North Carolina Press, 1951.

Woolley, Persia. *Child of the Northern Spring.* New York: Poseidon Books, 1987.

Woolley, Persia. *Queen of the Summer Stars.* New York: Poseidon Press, 1990.

About the Author

Tyler R. Tichelaar holds a Ph.D. in Literature from Western Michigan University, and Bachelor and Master's Degrees in English from Northern Michigan University. He has lectured on writing and literature at Clemson University, the University of Wisconsin, and the University of London. Tyler is the regular guest host of *Authors Access Internet Radio* and the current President of the Upper Peninsula Publishers and Authors Association. He is the owner of his own publishing company Marquette Fiction (www.Marquette Fiction.com) and Superior Book Promotions (www.SuperiorBook Promotions.com), a professional book review, editing, and proof-reading service.

Tichelaar is the author of five historical novels, *The Marquette Trilogy* (composed of *Iron Pioneers*, *The Queen City*, and *Superior Heritage*) as well as the award-winning *Narrow Lives* and *The Only Thing That Lasts*. He is also the author of *My Marquette* a personal history of his hometown. An avid genealogist, he has also been fascinated by the Arthurian legend and medieval history since childhood. He is currently working on *King Arthur's Legacy*, the first in a new series of historical novels focusing on legendary figures and King Arthur's descendants. For updates on Tyler R. Tichelaar's Arthurian novels, visit:

www.ChildrenOfArthur.com

Index

CPSIA information can be obtained at www.ICGtesting.com
Printed in the USA
LVOW101350120413

328884LV00001B/45/P